THE WHO'S TOMMY

THE MUSICAL

Music and Lyrics by Pete Townshend

Adapted for the stage by Pete Townshend and Des McAnuff

Photography by Peter Cunningham

DESIGN
Thomas K. Walker

EDITORIAL DIRECTION
Rita D. Jacobs

Produced by
KARDANA PRODUCTIONS and GRAF/x

Pantheon Books, New York

Grateful acknowledgment is made to the following for permis-
sion to reprint previously published material:
<u>The New York Times</u>: "Capturing Rock-and-Roll and the
Passions of 1969" by Frank Rich from the April 23, 1993 issue of
<u>The New York Times</u>. Copyright ©1993 by The New York Times
Company. Reprinted by permission.

Library of Congress Cataloging-in-Publication Data

Tommy [by] Pete Townshend: the musical.
p. cm.
Includes libretto.
ISBN 0-679-43066-0
1. Townshend, Pete. Who's Tommy. 2. Musicals—Production
and direction. 3. Musicals—Librettos. I. Townshend, Pete.
Who's Tommy. Libretto. 1993.
ML410.T69.T6 1993
782.1′4—dc20   93-21923
                                                          CIP
                                                          MN

Manufactured in the United States of America
First Edition
9 8 7 6 5 4 3 2 1

Contents

Tommy *is on Broadway. People love it and people hate it, but I am in a new kind of ecstasy. This current interest in what was a naive and impudent rock piece back in the late sixties has allowed me to reappraise my life as a writer. And I have learned there is a vital difference between the simple rock song and the conventional music theatre play—that it's necessary to bring a story to a conclusion, something you never have to do in rock-and-roll.*

The need to complete the story for music theatre is my new great challenge. Of course, I will always love to write a good rock song, with a loose ending, some poetry, some passion, some dreaming and even sometimes some impossible macho. But now that I'm in my late forties, it begins to feel insincere to pretend that I haven't arrived at any answers or drawn any conclusions. Because I have. My life has been and continues to be filled with vital experiences and the lessons that come with them.

This book attests to the fact that when you combine rock-and-roll with music theatre you have to start telling the complete truth. Here you see the director, his creative team, cast, musicians and author building a dream world. And despite the fact that all of these people speak the truth and reveal that the dream is made of flesh, glue and string, it still feels enchanting. I for one, with a nod of my addictive rock-and-roll personality to Des McAnuff, who warned me it would happen, have to admit I am totally hooked on music theatre and all that goes with it.

Pete Townshend

25 Years of *Tommy*

Ira Robbins

"**I**t's a girl, Mrs. Walker, it's a girl." Despite the gender discrepancy, that lyric—the coda of "Glow Girl," a shelved Who song from early 1968—was the first recorded breath drawn by a character destined to become a prodigious rock-and-roll figure. Tommy, the deaf, dumb and blind boy, star of album, concert stage, screen and now Broadway, was born with a musical theme in his mouth—the four-strum guitar figure and dramatic descending riff first used in a 1967 album track, "Rael." (Incidentally, "I Can't Reach You," another song on *The Who Sell Out*, contains the lyrics "…see, feel or hear from ya.")

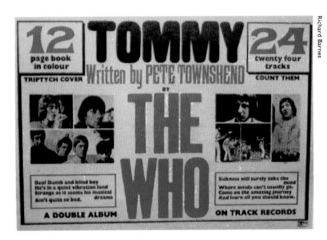

Like many young British rockers of his generation, Pete Townshend took musical cues from choice American R&B and rock stars (James Brown, Bo Diddley, the Motown stable, Eddie Cochran) as well as homegrown interpreters of same (Rolling Stones, Yardbirds, Beatles). The group began as a West London (Shepherd's Bush) five-piece known as the Detours; the arrival of Keith Moon fit the final piece into what became the classic foursome, initially renamed the High Numbers, of Roger Daltrey, John Alec Entwistle, Townshend and Moon. Manager Pete Meaden groomed the young quartet to become the chosen heroes of the trendy Mod crowd. They dressed in tight-fitting clothes with bold, pop-art designs, danced the latest steps and curried favor among the "faces," as the scene's hippest kids were known. Meaden rewrote a popular Slim Harpo song for the band's first single, "I'm the Face," but it was released in mid-1964 to little notice.

Would-be filmmakers Kit Lambert and Chris Stamp took over the group's management later that year. The pair matched the band's blazing music with their own audacious promotional schemes, and set the now-renamed Who on an inevitable course to global fame. The Who took up a Tuesday night residency at London's Marquee Club, using the "Maximum R&B" slogan, and quickly became the talk of the town as the group that broke all the conventional rules (such as they stood) of rock-and-roll politesse. By January 1965, when "I Can't Explain" became the Who's first single and hit, the juggernaut was rolling.

The Who's explosive guitarist turned 19 and was just beginning to write songs in 1964. Within the group's first year, however, he had delivered two enduring rock classics. "I Can't Explain" and "My Generation," both songs of unmistakable strength and originality, only hinted at Townshend's enormous potential, but they quickly marked the Who as purvey-

Left: Pete Townshend, The Cow Palace, San Francisco, 1967 (Photo: Baron Wolman).

Below: The Who (Keith Moon, John Entwistle, Roger Daltrey, Pete Townshend) 1965.

ors of Top 40 singles, a limiting perception that gave the group a barrier to struggle against. On the Who's sophomore album, a career point at which many of the era's groups remained timidly rooted to safe repetition, Townshend—quick to credit Who manager Kit Lambert for pushing the idea—strung together seven musical segments to produce the nine-minute "A Quick One While He's Away," a lighthearted morality play that used giddy background vocals chanting "cello, cello"

for mock classical pretense. Without spurning the self-contained pop single or drifting into the vapid trap of extended improvisational indulgence, Townshend began exploring the structural challenge of constructing longer narrative pieces.

In 1967, inspired by his devotion to the writings of Indian guru Meher Baba (cited as Avatar in *Tommy*'s sleeve credits), Townshend poured out a long, deeply reflective stream-of-consciousness poem entitled "Amazing Journey" which contained the essence of Tommy's pivotal song. From that conceptual base, Townshend began to literally graph out an intricate tale of sensual deprivation and spiritual enlightenment. To that metaphysical stew, he added a dose of anti-authoritarianism, with observations on the cruel ironies of pop fame, pop fandom and false messiahs, the visionary conceit of psychedelic drugs, postwar Britain, dysfunctional families and, oddly enough, pinball. (Nik Cohn, the British rock critic who was an early and articulate champion of the Who and a crony of Townshend's, wrote a contemporaneous novel entitled *Arfur, Teenage Pinball Queen*.) For his figurative stand-in, "Each sensation [made] a note in his symphony"; for Townshend, every idea became a song in his rock opera.

Material flowed in and out of the project's unfixed frame for more than a year. "She's a Sensation," a song about someone Townshend met while on tour in Australia, was switched to the first person and bestowed on Tommy. After a New York concert the Who played with the Doors in the summer of '68 ended in a minor riot, Townshend chronicled the hazards of fan hysteria in a number that became "Sally Simpson." Bassist John Entwistle, the composer of such darkly amusing Who items as "Boris the Spider" and "Dr. Jekyll and Mr. Hyde," tackled the tale's two characters—pedophiliac Uncle Ernie and malicious Cousin Kevin—who required his deliciously sinister outlook. As the story took final shape, lyrics were altered to fit: Townshend's homemade demo tape of "Go the Mirror," for instance, differs substantially from the finished album track.

In June 1968, Who vocalist Roger Daltrey announced that the group would soon begin recording a "rock-and-roll opera, possibly running as long as two hours." Two months later, Jann Wenner, the editor of *Rolling Stone,* listened as Townshend outlined the concept of what was then called *Deaf, Dumb and Blind Boy.* But it wasn't until the following spring, after six months of concentrated studio effort (and numerous working titles), that the Who would actually unveil their extraordinary undertaking.

The Fillmore East, New York City, May 16, 1969. Pete Townshend waves a copy of *Tommy* over his head and idly asks the cheering crowd if they've heard the band's new record yet. "Pinball Wizard," the double album's initial single, had been on the radio for a month, but the album was just then arriving in record stores, so many hadn't. Regardless, the Who set about ripping through the bulk of *Tommy* in

Above: The Who, London, 1965.

Right: The Who, San Francisco, 1967.

Below: The Who in concert, 1966.

Baron Wolman

a typically overpowering performance. Louder than hell, these four autonomous auteurs, bound together in coordinated planetary alignment, produced an overpowering force of music. With his trademark windmill strumming and gravity defying leaps, Pete Townshend led the charge, vaulting into improvisational regions where the others easily, intuitively, joined him. Before the final explosion, in which Townshend would frequently wind himself up to a level of tension that demanded the sacrifice of a Gibson SG (or some other doomed guitar), the set ended abruptly with the evacuation of the smoke-filled theater (due to a terrorist fire set next door) and the arrest of Pete Townshend for his climactic, and well-executed, booting of a plainclothes policeman who had rushed onstage and, without explanation, grabbed the mike out of Daltrey's hand.

If *Tommy*'s plot was incomprehensible to the Fillmore crowd, it didn't matter. The songs meshed stylistically with the rest of the Who's live repertoire (numbers like "My Generation" and "Substitute"), and there would be plenty of time the next day to buy the album and apprehend the action, a convoluted fantasy very much in the searching-for-truth-in-the-youth-nation spirit of the late sixties, but cleanly cut with a healthy dose of nonutopian skepticism. Beyond its intrinsic merits, this carefully constructed piece of music was virtually unprecedented in the rock universe. Previous concept albums, like the Pretty Things' *S.F. Sorrow* and, of course, *Sgt. Pepper's Lonely Hearts Club Band,* did not even attempt to sustain a detailed, cohesive plot over four sides of electrifying vinyl.

MCA Records/Cover design by Mike McInnerney

The Who had been something of a poorly kept secret in America up until the release of *Tommy*. Despite a handful of hit singles and a certain underground credibility, the quartet's notoriety for on- and offstage destruction, not to mention records about transvestitism, masturbation, drugs and deodorant had not entirely endeared the Who to the entirety of rock's vast teen audience. Like the Rolling Stones, the Who were not altogether respectable, even in the disreputable realm of rock. *Tommy*, which reached number 4 in *Billboard* and went gold, changed everything.

While some hasty critics pilloried the album as a "sick" tale of psychosomatic illness, noting its intimations of child molestation, sadism and LSD/sex therapy, one

WHO FACTS

- The Who were approached to appear in *Blow-Up* (1966), but the job went to the Yardbirds, whose guitarist, Jeff Beck, destroyed a guitar in tribute to Townshend.

- The instrumental B-side to the "Substitute" single, credited to the Who orchestra, is in fact by the unrelated Graham Bond Organization.

- Keith Moon once emceed a Sha Na Na concert (at Carnegie Hall, no less) in full drag, complete with bouffant wig, lamé dress and cigarette holder.

- Cover versions recorded by the Who: "The Batman Theme," "Heatwave," "Barbara Ann" and "Summertime Blues." In 1967, the Who cut two Rolling Stones' songs for a 45 protesting the drug convictions of Mick Jagger and Keith Richards.

- In 1973, at a Who concert in San Francisco, Keith Moon collapsed, and a fan named Scott Halpin sat in for him.

- Keith Moon was once rumored to be joining the Beach Boys.

—*I.R.*

13

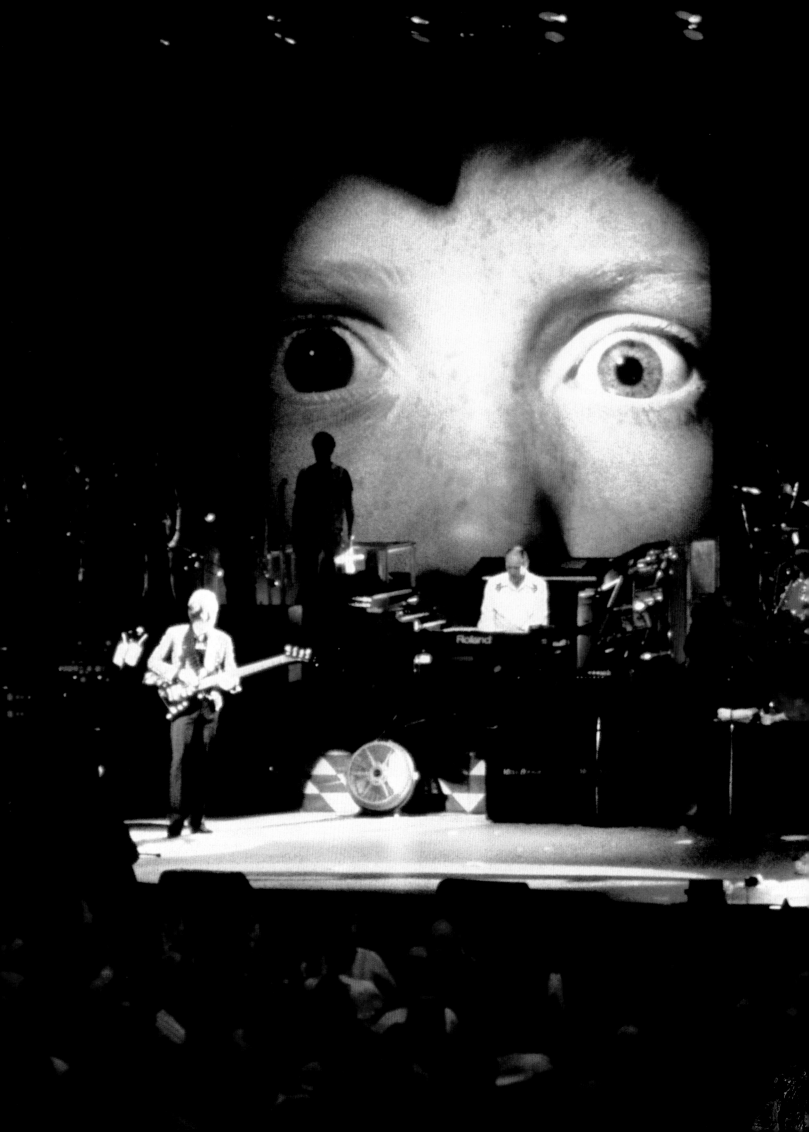

Christian reviewer praised its religiosity. *Billboard* enthused in obscure trade language: "…plenty of instrumentals make this package a hot item." The *New York Times* was more forthright in its effusion: "This just might be the first pop master-

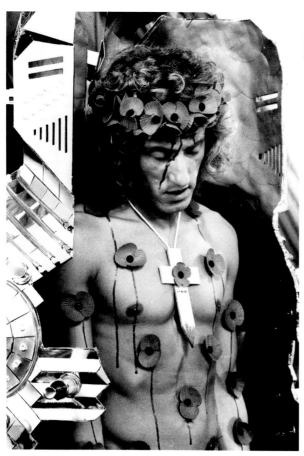

piece." While acknowledging the presence of a proper overture, restated themes, narrative instrumental passages and other formal conventions in *Tommy*, classical buffs rebuffed its characterization as "rock opera," counter-offering such designations as cantata or song cycle. (Townshend declined the debate. "I didn't need the music critics to tell me it wasn't an opera.") In any case, as one observer later reflected, *Tommy* gave the Who what every success story needs: a hook. The Who became "the group with the rock opera."

That handle provided the ticket to elevate the Who from mortal rock band to near-mythic status. While the high-brow pretension of liking a "rock opera" flattered rock fans and lent them intellectual ammunition in the era's generation-gap debate over the artistic validity of youth culture, *Tommy* required no actual knowledge or concern for classical music or composition. Nothing in *Tommy* challenged rock's essential parameters. John Entwistle's French horn playing (already an occasional Who element) added a mild upper-crust accent to the proceedings, but otherwise *Tommy*'s music

Roger Daltrey in Ken Russell's movie *Tommy*, 1975.

stuck to the Who's familiar amalgam of guitar, bass, drums and, lately, keyboards. Despite prodding, the Who refused any outside assistance, which precluded the string quartet, guest vocalists or other embellishments Kit Lambert might have encouraged. Nor did the group grant any ground to nonrock sensibilities. The sophisticated sound of *Tommy* reflected the Who's natural maturation progress, but it was unquestionably a rock album from one of rock's most dynamic, forceful outfits. The amplifiers stayed fully on, Daltrey—who, as the band's onstage front man, would become the embodiment of Tommy—sang with all his might and the irrepressible Keith Moon drummed up his usual hyperactive storm. While Townshend could collect kudos for the scope of his conceptual feat and controversy for its format, each one of the album's two dozen songs (save for the thirty-four fleeting seconds of "Miracle Cure" and "There's a Doctor I've Found") could stand firmly on its own. Only when taken as a collective work did the story of Tommy— and what a vague, ambiguous story it is, subject to manifold interpretations, both literal and figurative, by author and listener alike—unfold.

The album brought the Who acclaim, chart-climbing sales and a taste of the financial security they had previously lacked. The Who spent the remainder of 1969 performing their opus across Europe and America, highlighted by an August appearance at the Woodstock Festival and a record-breaking six-night stand back at the Fillmore, complete with libretto, intermission and psychedelic light show. Then it was on to a short 1970 tour of selected Continental opera houses, followed by a prestigious, tradition-smashing date at the Met in New York, where the Who broke their own performing precedent and managed two exhausting back-to-back shows on a single Sunday. *Tommy* and the Who were becoming synonymous in the public mind, and it began to appear that the group might find it very difficult to move forward without that famous Walker boy in tow.

Although the brouhaha over *Tommy*'s artistic allegiance quickly subsided—playing opera houses finally underscored how tenuous the opera connection was—impresarios from both sides of the rock divide continued to stake claims on its split identity by mounting a variety of creative efforts. *Tommy* proved to be a hardy lad, enduring one approach after another. Les Grands Ballet Canadiens toured a terpsichorean interpretation in 1971, using the actual Who album as its score. The Seattle Opera Association presented *Tommy,* with Bette Midler singing the parts of Mrs. Walker and the Acid Queen. Productions also took place in Los Angeles and Atlanta, London and Leicester.

Artwork from the London Symphony Orchestra recording of *Tommy*.

Tommy went off to play with his new friends around the world, and the Who took no further part in the album's afterlife—until American record producer Lou Reizner proposed a full-fledged orchestral treatment. Reizner obtained Townshend's blessing to record (and later stage) *Tommy* with the London Symphony Orchestra and Chambre Choir and an all-star cast of featured vocalists like Steve Winwood, Ringo Starr and Rod Stewart. Released on Ode Records only three years after the original, this grandiose effort—which once seemed pompous and stylistically traitorous—now sounds quite legitimate and, if anything, positively underscores the achievement of the Who's self-contained original (which, in America, it nearly outsold). Bits of *Tommy* began turning up in record racks with alarming frequency. The instrumental "Overture from `Tommy'" was a big 1970 hit for the Assembled Multitude; the New Seekers grafted "Pinball Wizard" onto "See Me Feel Me" for a 1973 chart single. In the LSO's wake, a one-disc knockoff, *Tommy: Excerpts from the Rock Opera,* was released, starring British session singer Tony Rivers in the title role. Later a Philadelphia studio crew trotted out synthesizers for the ludicrous technoinstrumental *Electric Tommy* (Chelsea).

But none of these puny revisionists could hold a candle to the singular vision of film director Ken Russell. Increasingly burdened by what was already a

All-star *Tommy* performance (including Billy Idol as Cousin Kevin, Patti LaBelle as the Acid Queen, Elton John as the Pinball Wizard, Robert Plant as the Hawker and Phil Collins as Uncle Ernie), Los Angeles, 1989.

WHO CHRONOLOGY

1962: Pete Townshend and John Entwistle join Roger Daltrey's band The Detours.

1964: Keith Moon joins the Who. Briefly renamed the High Numbers, they release their first single, "I'm the Face."

1965: The Who releases its first single, " I Can't Explain"; it reaches the Top 10 in the U.K. and the Top 100 in America.

1966: *The Who Sings My Generation* brings the group to American LP racks for the first time. The names of both Entwistle and Daltrey are misspelled on the back cover.

1967: The Who plays a Murray The K package show in New York and the Monterey Pop Festival before touring the U.S. as Herman's Hermits' opening act. Albums: *Happy Jack* (another bonus "h" in Entwistle) and *The Who Sell Out.*

1969: *Tommy,* the record. Woodstock. "Pinball Wizard." Townshend produces and plays bass on Thunderclap Newman's hit, "Something in the Air."

1970: *Live at Leeds.* The Who performs *Tommy* in opera houses from Paris to Copenhagen to West Berlin and finally goes to New York's Metropolitan Opera House. The single "The Seeker" follows. The ambitious *Lifehouse* project doesn't succeed, but does produce several of the Who's most famous songs, including their definitive arena anthems "Won't Get Fooled Again" and "Baba O'Riley."

1971: *Who's Next* elevates the Who to top-ranking classic-rock arena attraction. John Entwistle finds time to make a solo album, *Smash Your Head Against the Wall.*

1972: Townshend releases his first solo album, *Who Came First.* Entwistle issues his second. *Tommy,* the London Symphony Orchestra version, bows.

1973: The Who releases another two-disc concept album, *Quadrophenia.* Daltrey sings himself a solo record.

1975: *Tommy,* the movie by Ken Russell, opens, starring Jack Nicholson in his first singing role, along with Ann-Margret, Elton John and Tina Turner. Pete Townshend is nominated for an Oscar for best adaptation of a musical score. *The Who by Numbers* appears. John Entwistle takes his side band, John Entwistle's Ox, on the road. Keith Moon becomes the fourth member to issue a solo album.

1977: Pete Townshend and Ronnie Lane (ex-Small Faces/Faces) release their collaborative album, *Rough Mix.*

1978: Issued in August, *Who Are You* becomes the original group's final album when Moon dies in September.

1979: The *Quadrophenia* film opens, as does *The Kids Are Alright* documentary. Kenney Jones becomes the Who's drummer. Catastrophe in Cincinnati: eleven fans die at Who concert.

1980: Daltrey the actor stars in *McVicar;* Townshend the solo act proffers his best-selling album, *Empty Glass.*

1981: Kit Lambert, the Who's former manager and producer, dies after falling down a flight of stairs.

1982: Final Who album, *It's Hard,* and farewell tour.

1985: Townshend assembles a live band (Deep End) and plays solo. The Who reunites for Live Aid.

1988: The Who gets together and performs for the British Music Industry Awards broadcast.

1989: 25th Anniversary reunion tour climaxes with full-scale stagings of *Tommy* in New York and Los Angeles.

1990: The Who are inducted into the Rock-and-Roll Hall of Fame.

1992: A theatrical incarnation of *Tommy* is produced in La Jolla, California.

1993: *Tommy* reaches Broadway, winning five Tonys, including one for Pete Townshend for best original score.

—I.R.

distant piece of Who history, Townshend may have seen a major motion picture as the way to leave *Tommy* behind, once and for all. (There had been talk of turning the cameras on *Tommy* as early as 1969; the film opened in 1975.) Sounding like a parent anxious to see his child leave the nest in the worst possible way, Townshend recklessly encouraged Russell: "I told [him] I didn't care if he altered all the words if he needed to: 'Listening to you I get the porridge…'"

The director's grand plans didn't seem unduly hampered by anything so insignificant as lyrics (or budgets), and the movie, at his bidding, went over the top in all directions at once. (The lavish premiere party, held in a New York City subway station, was not atypical of the enterprise.) Townshend came up with a pair of new songs ("Mother and Son," "Champagne") documented on the rerecorded soundtrack but unincorporated into any further *Tommy* incarnations. Working from Russell's own script, a colorful cast of actors and rock stars—Roger Daltrey, Ann-Margret, Oliver Reed, Eric Clapton, Tina Turner, Elton John, Jack Nicholson—filled the screen with extravagant set pieces, singing in the most bizarre circumstances Russell could concoct. Typical of the decade's wildly overstimulated pop-culture delusions, advertisements promised "Your senses will never be the same."

Pete Townshend, China Club, New York, 1993.

If nothing else, the Who would never be the same. New doors opened to them, individually and collectively. The group gained a vast new audience too young or un-rock-conscious to have otherwise known much of their work. Daltrey, who seized the title role as an unparalleled chance to make the transition from music to drama, won praise for his performance as Tommy and launched a successful sideline in films (*Lisztomania*, *McVicar*) and television (*The Beggar's Opera*).

Lofted into the rarefied stratosphere of mass-media power, the Who became less a rock-and-roll band and more a loud entertainment organization. Solo careers moved forward as the band toured and recorded less, especially after Keith Moon's death. (Following a star-studded party thrown by Paul McCartney on September 6, 1978, the drummer overdosed on prescription drugs and alcohol.) Retiring after a huge farewell tour in 1982, the three surviving members reunited in 1989 for a twenty-fifth-anniversary outing that culminated in grand performances of *Tommy* in New York and Los Angeles (where Phil Collins, Billy Idol and, in a memorable turn as the Acid Queen, Patti LaBelle participated in a pay-per-view cable extravaganza preserved on home video) to benefit several charities. Throughout the tour, the Who—joined by a stage full of supporting musicians and singers—sought to reclaim an older, well-traveled *Tommy*. Townshend's creation had proven to be as tangible and indomitable as any corporeal rock legend.

With such a swan song unlikely to be repeated, the Who's reunion tour appeared to be *Tommy*'s final curtain call. Or so it seemed, until word seeped out that Townshend was involved in a theatrical project being developed in La Jolla, California. Is there an ending to this story? *Tommy*'s been through a lot, but there's still life left in the old boy, as was proved at the St. James Theatre on April 22, 1993.

Ira Robbins is co-founder of Trouser Press and pop music editor of New York Newsday.

ACT 1

THE YEAR IS 1940. AGAINST THE BACKDROP OF WORLD WAR II appears a montage of the Walkers' meeting, courtship, marriage, Capt. Walker's departure for the front and his capture and internment in a POW camp. The scene shifts to London where two officers arrive at 22 Heathfield Gardens to bring Mrs. Walker the tragic news that her husband did not return. The following year a nurse gently hands Mrs. Walker her newborn son.

1945: Capt. Walker is freed and heads home, arriving as Mrs. Walker is celebrating her birthday with her lover and four-year-old son. Looking in a mirror, Tommy sees the furious Capt. Walker shoot and kill the lover. The Walkers realize what Tommy has witnessed and vehemently tell him to forget everything he's seen and heard. The police arrive to investigate while Tommy just stares at his own reflection. The Narrator—Tommy's older self—appears, visible only to Tommy. The scene shifts to a courtroom where Capt. Walker is found not guilty, but the family celebration dies out as they realize Tommy is now deaf, dumb and blind. The Walkers take Tommy to a hospital for examination.

1950: The Walkers take ten-year-old Tommy to church and to a family Christmas dinner where he responds to Uncle Ernie's French horn playing and to the older Tommy's unseen presence. Back home the Walkers worry about leaving Tommy with drunken Uncle Ernie, who, once alone with Tommy, molests him. Tommy's next baby-sitter, Cousin Kevin, taunts him mercilessly and then takes him to the youth club where, to everyone's astonishment, Tommy plays pinball brilliantly.

Encouraged, the Walkers try another doctor who tests Tommy without success. The Hawker approaches Capt. Walker and promises a miracle cure through a prostitute, the Gypsy, but Mr. Walker ends up snatching the boy away in horror. The act ends in 1958 as a group of youths eagerly await the teenaged Tommy at the amusement arcade. The Narrator and Tommy are now one.

OVERTURE

PROLOGUE: 1940. Against the black-and-white backdrop of a gigantic bomber and the projection of a factory workers' propaganda poster ("Speed Is Vital"), a welder is at work, face hidden behind a welding mask, on a Royal Air Force bomber. A flight crew appears, followed by Capt. Walker, a handsome Englishman in his mid-twenties. His path being blocked by a fuel hose, he stands behind the welder. Sparks fly. Trying to get the welder's attention, Capt. Walker pats the welder on the back. The welder turns, stands, and flips back the mask, pulls the cap off and wipes the sweat away. Hair spills down around her shoulders. Capt. Walker stares at the young woman. He smiles. (GO TO THE MIRROR) Another factory poster is seen ("Come to the Factories") and RAF officers and young Englishwomen appear wildly doing the jitterbug on a smoke-filled dance floor. Uncle Ernie, Capt. Walker's older brother, dressed in civilian clothes (he has a slight limp) watches the dancers, grins, sips his tea as Capt. Walker and the welder, now in party dress, whirl across the room. (SEE ME, FEEL ME) The group of officers and women separate and magically Capt. Walker and the welder are revealed, he still in uniform, she in a simple white dress. A minister performs the wedding ceremony against the backdrop of a church.

MINISTER
The union of husband and wife in heart, body and mind is intended by God for their mutual joy; for the help and comfort given one another in prosperity and adversity; and, when it is God's will, for the procreation of children and their nurture in the knowledge and love of the Lord. Therefore marriage is not to be entered into unadvisedly or lightly, but reverently, deliberately, and in accordance with the purposes for which it was instituted by God.

Uncle Ernie walks up, stands by Capt. Walker's side and hands him a ring. Capt. Walker impatiently places the ring on Mrs. Walker's finger and kisses her passionately in silhouette. (GO TO THE MIRROR) Air Raid sirens go off as aerial shots of London in the blitz appear in the background. Uncle Ernie produces a civil defense armband, which he dons, and a flashlight. We hear the drone of the engines of bombers overhead as searchlights flash in the background to the sound of nearby explosions. Uncle Ernie hurries off. (LISTENING TO YOU) Mrs. Walker is in bed, asleep. Distant explosions. Capt. Walker leans over and kisses her softly. She stirs but doesn't awaken. He watches her for a moment longer and then quietly creeps away. (FRENCH HORN FANFARE) Against a giant propaganda poster of Winston Churchill, Capt. Walker arrives at the airfield where he is helped into his combat uniform by an aide who fastens a parachute on the Captain's back. Airborne troops perform exercises at the edge of the airfield. (PINBALL WIZARD) Two

rows of soldiers sit on benches facing each other in the hull of a Wellington bomber, where Capt. Walker joins them. In flight, bursts of antiaircraft shells explode around them. A trap door opens; flames from far below are reflected on the faces of the soldiers as, one by one, the soldiers step to the edge of the trap and leap into the abyss. Capt. Walker is the last to jump.

Projections of parachutes fill the sky in a Magritte-like image. A figure slowly descends from above, suspended under his chute—Capt. Walker. Two German footsoldiers stare up at the sky. They raise machine guns in the air and fire. There is the deafening sound of the rounds going off as the lights black out.

A series of aerial shots of London take us from the black-and-white world of the prologue to the warm faded colors of remembered suburbia.

SCENE 1: 22 HEATHFIELD GARDENS, 1941

———————•———————

(A very pleased Uncle Ernie knocks on a simple white door marked "22" which is answered by Mrs. Walker in a dressing gown.)

UNCLE ERNIE
Sardines! An egg! Un demi-litre du lait!

MRS. WALKER
Bless you, Ernie!

(As Ernie is leaving, he passes two RAF officers coming to the door.)

"The idea of the flyers parachuting out of the Wellington bomber was cooked up very early in planning the show. I love the fact that the kind of trap door through which the actors disappear is hundreds of years old—in the nineteenth century they used to call them vampires."

—Des McAnuff, Director

CAPTAIN WALKER

FIRST OFFICER *(to audience)*
>
> Capt. Walker didn't come home.
> His unborn child will never know him.

SECOND OFFICER *(to Mrs. Walker)*
>
> Believe him missing with a number of men.
> Don't expect to see him again.

(The officer presents Mrs. Walker with an official paper informing her that Capt. Walker is missing-in-action.)

FIRST & SECOND OFFICERS
>
> Capt. Walker didn't come home.
> Capt. Walker didn't come home.
> Capt. Walker didn't come home.
> His unborn child will never know him.

(Mrs. Walker goes back into the house in shock. To comfort him one of the officers presses a pint of whiskey into the teetotaling Uncle Ernie's hand. He gives it a try.)

(A background of graveyard crosses is transformed into a prison camp, where a lone prisoner, Capt. Walker, walks.)

"Projections are more than just a replacement for painted drops because they're a fluid, animated medium. When the images change or move there's a demand for intellectual engagement on the part of the audience—almost a request asking them to come along with the images."

—Wendall Harrington, Projection Designer

SCENE 2: HOSPITAL

———•———

(Mrs. Walker is pushed along in a wheelchair by a nurse. Another nurse carries a small bundle which she gently presents to Mrs. Walker.)

IT'S A BOY

NURSE   It's a boy, Mrs. Walker, it's a boy.

NURSES   It's a boy, Mrs. Walker, it's a boy.

MRS. WALKER & THE NURSES
    A son! A son! A son!

(In the foreground Uncle Ernie continues to drink against projections of barbed wire. Capt. Walker sits behind the metal gates of a prison camp as the years go by from 1942 to 1945; Allied soldiers rush in to liberate the camp.)

ALLIED SOLDIER No. 1
    Back home they're celebrating in the streets,
    And freedom reigns on this first day of peace.

CAPT. WALKER & SOLDIERS
    We've won! We've won! We've won!

(The soldiers help Capt. Walker off as the pieces of his home in London assemble.)

> **"The one constant for me in the show is that
> it's about a mother's unconditional love for
> her child and what that commitment means.
> No matter what the circumstances, she's
> ready to accept Tommy."**
>
> —Marcia Mitzman, *Mrs. Walker*

SCENE 3: 22 HEATHFIELD GARDENS, 1945

———•———

(Mrs. Walker is celebrating her twenty-first birthday with her four-year-old son, Tommy, and her new lover. With his shirt off and very much at home, the Lover watches as Tommy impatiently waits for his piece of cake.)

TWENTY-ONE

MRS. WALKER *(to her lover)*
> Gotta feelin' twenty-one
> Is gonna be a good year…
> Especially if you and me
> See it in together.

LOVER *(to Mrs. Walker)*
> Now you're twenty-one
> You're ready for a new year.
> Let's marry now
> And celebrate forever.

MRS. WALKER   I had no reason to be overoptimistic,
> But somehow when you smile
> I can brave bad weather.

> Gotta feelin' twenty-one
> Is gonna be a good year…

LOVER   Twenty-one today—
> Your future is with me now.
> … Especially if you and me
> See it in together.
> Our future is your freedom.

(Mrs. Walker takes Tommy back into the bedroom, where he gives her a flower.)

> Now you're twenty-one
> Only twenty-one today
> You're ready for a new year.
> And I've such a grown-up son.
> Let's marry now
> Wish your Mum a happy day!
> And celebrate forever.

FOUR-YEAR-OLD TOMMY
Happy Birthday, Mum.

"Little Tommy starts out in a white nightshirt and from that point on Tommy wears white. He's the innocent and then he turns into a sort of spiritual leader, and we thought that white would underscore his purity which is so central to the play."

—David Woolard, *Costume Designer*

MRS. WALKER (*to Tommy*)
> I had no reason to be overoptimistic,
> But somehow when you smile
> I can brave bad weather.

(*Mrs. Walker kisses Tommy goodnight and comes back into the front room, where her lover waits for her with champagne.*)

MRS. WALKER & LOVER
> I had no reason to be overoptimistic,
> But somehow when you smile
> I can brave bad weather.

(*INSTRUMENTAL*) *Returning unexpectedly from the war, Capt. Walker appears at the door late at night to find Mrs. Walker and her lover in an embrace. The Lover attacks Capt. Walker, and the four-year-old Tommy is woken up by the commotion. Mrs. Walker tries to turn him away from the violent scene, but he faces a mirror in which he witnesses the Lover slapping his mother and threatening to attack his father with a chair. The father shoots the Lover in the head. The Walkers embrace, helplessly, then realize that Tommy has seen it all in the mirror.*

YOU DIDN'T HEAR IT

MRS. WALKER   What about the boy?

CAPT. WALKER   What about the boy?

BOTH   What about the boy?
                 He saw it all!

> You didn't hear it,
> You didn't see it,
> You won't say nothing to no one
> Ever in your life.
> You never heard it.
> How absurd it'll
> Seem without any proof.

Ken Russell's *Tommy*   1975

THE CONFLICT BETWEEN LOVER AND FATHER ALWAYS HAD A clear resolution in Pete Townshend's mind. "I never had any doubt that the Lover died. The family that remains must be a family by blood rather than adoption in order for the parents' shame and responsibility for Tommy's trauma to be properly and deeply felt. I don't think it's enough to feel that they are upset because they created an incident in which he witnessed a murder and slid into what appears to be autism. I think they have to feel his response is genetically rooted—they are to 'blame' as biological parents, too.

"Ken Russell wanted the father to be sacrificed, iconized. There are good arguments for why that can work; after all, as far as Tommy is concerned, the Lover has been a surrogate father to him and his biological father has been away a long time. From Tommy's point of view, it doesn't seem to make much difference. Where it does make a difference is in the way we the audience feel about how the parents must feel. In the film we don't care that much. In the current musical I think we do."

"*I've been in prison camp for four years, I come home, my wife's there with another man and I have a child. All of a sudden, there's an argument and somebody's dead. It's surreal and bizarre and all of the shock gets focused on little Tommy.*

"That whole moment is about being desperate, drowning in confusion and clinging to something. In this case, we've pulled Tommy under water, and even though we're going to come out of it, he remains submerged."

—Jonathan Dokuchitz, *Captain Walker*

You didn't hear it,
You didn't see it,
You never heard it, not a word of it.
You won't say nothing to no one.
Never tell a soul
What you know is the...

You didn't hear it,
You didn't see it,
You won't say nothing to no one
Ever in your life.
You never heard it.
How absurd it'll
Seem without any...

You didn't hear it,
You didn't see it,
You never heard it, not a word of it.
You won't say nothing to no one.
Never tell a soul
What you know is the truth.

CAPT. WALKER   What about the boy?

(Police pour onto the scene, examine the body and take Mr. Walker into custody.)

MRS. WALKER
Tommy. Everything's going to be alright. Do you understand?

(Tommy doesn't respond.)

MRS. WALKER
You needn't be afraid, love. Tommy? Do you hear me?

(Tommy doesn't answer.)

MRS. WALKER
Tommy, do you understand Mummy?

(Tommy walks to the mirror on the wardrobe. The objects he sees in it seem to defy the laws of gravity and space. A chair flies into the air. Doors take on new positions. The view outside the windows becomes scrambled.)

MRS. WALKER
Tommy! Tommy!

(Tommy just stares at the mirror. The police separate the Walkers for questioning while the older Tommy, our Narrator, appears on top of the wardrobe as if by magic.)

AMAZING JOURNEY

TOMMY   Deaf, dumb and blind boy…
He's in a quiet vibration land.
Strange as it seems, his musical dreams
Ain't quite so bad.

Four years old
With thoughts as bold as thought can be;
Loving life and becoming wise
In simplicity.

Sickness will surely take the mind
Where minds can't usually go.
Come on the amazing journey
And learn all you should know.

A vague haze of delirium
Seeps in his mind.
Soaring and flying images blind.

I'll be your leader;
I'll be your guide.
On the amazing journey, together we'll ride.

Nothing to say,
Nothing to hear,
Nothing to see.
Each sensation makes a note in his symphony.

Sickness will surely take the mind
Where minds can't usually go.
Come on the amazing journey
And learn all you should know.

His eyes are the eyes that
Transmit all they know.
The truth burns so bright
It can melt winter snow.
A towering figure,
So brilliant, so high…
A white sun burning
The earth and the sky.

(The Narrator vanishes and the house disassembles.)

THE BOOK OF THE MUSICAL ACTUALLY REFLECTS ONE OF Pete Townshend's early visions of Tommy. "It became clear early in the book work that we needed our older Tommy to be present from the start of the show. In a very early treatment for the original album, I explained the story by using the device of two converging pathways—the crossroads being the moment of freedom. On one pathway we saw the progress of the mortal Tommy, growing up, growing wise, growing old and dying. On the other pathway, we saw the immortal soul of Tommy, ageless, innocent and powerful. The first song I wrote for Tommy was 'Amazing Journey,' in which I described what the latter (internal, spiritual) Tommy was experiencing. This left almost the entire opera to tell the rest of the external story. Des loved this idea and developed it theatrically."

SCENE 4: AN ENGLISH COURTROOM, 1945

———•———

(Against the background of a huge Union Jack, the Walker family stands to await the judge's verdict. Capt. Walker, still in uniform, is in the prisoner's docket.)

JUDGE
Capt. Walker, after much consideration, on the grounds of justifiable homicide, this court finds you… Not Guilty.

(There is elation in the courtroom, but Tommy doesn't move.)

JUDGE
Little boy, your parents have had some very good news indeed. I hope you can appreciate that fact.

(There is no response from Tommy. The flag seems to melt. The words spoken to him by grown-ups start to seem like some sinister, unrecognizable, otherworldly language.)

JUDGE
Little boy, what about a small smile in celebration of this most happy turn of events?

FIRST BARRISTER
Do you hear, my boy? The magistrate is speaking to you!

SECOND BARRISTER
Young Master Walker appears to be under a certain amount of strain, Your Honour.

(As he becomes the center of attention, Tommy just stares blankly ahead.)

MRS. WALKER
My God, Tommy… what ever is happening to you, my love?

(The Walkers kneel by Tommy and begin to realize what they may have done to their son. As Uncle Ernie sneaks a shot out of a flask, they lead Tommy off to get medical help.)

"The courtroom is where the characters first notice Tommy's traumatic state. To bring about that same recognition in the audience, we simulated little Tommy's state of mind by using a Lexicon effects processor to create eerie voice echoes at the same time as the slide-projected background was becoming distorted."

—Steve Canyon Kennedy, *Sound Designer*

McAnuff Stages a Classic Coup

In addition to being the director and coauthor with Pete Townshend of the Broadway musical Tommy, *Des McAnuff is the artistic director of the La Jolla Playhouse, where this version of* Tommy *first appeared on stage in June 1992.*

Directing *Tommy* is a great deal like directing a classic—something that people have either read or seen performed before. And in a way, *Tommy* may carry even more baggage than a classic drama because the original album was less specific. Every listener's imagination could evolve the story in a particular and disparate direction.

With *Tommy* there is the additional complication of dealing with people's fantasies based on early emotional experiences. It's in their teens that most people find their genre, and once you marry yourself to a genre, if you indeed do, it affects you profoundly for the rest of your life. The experience of discovering your own generation and what unites you can be really powerful.

That was true of *Tommy* for me.

I first heard the album in the summer of 1969. I was seventeen, in high school and in love with both the theatre and rock-and-roll. *Tommy* struck me right away with its inherent theatricality and story—even though the story was a little bit sketchy. It also had at its core a strong and perhaps profound notion, which was that you could put a deaf, dumb and blind child at the center of a contemporary fable.

Moreover, the music was far more exciting to me than any of the rock-and-roll music in theatre up to that time, for example, in musicals like *Your Own Thing.* When *Hair* came along and *Tommy* was issued, I realized that I could have everything I loved in the theatre.

This is actually the deep background for the moment years later when Michael David told me on July 15, 1991, that PACE Theatrical Group had approached Dodger Productions about doing some kind of version of *Tommy.* When he asked what I thought, I remembered a piece I had read by the critic for the *L.A. Times,* Dan Sullivan, who had reviewed the concert version that the Who did in 1989. He had posed the question "Why has nobody ever done this as the quintessential rock musical?" and basically came up with the following answer: "I guess it's because nobody could really capture the excitement, the event, of rock-and-roll."

I had often wondered myself why there'd never been a fully staged theatrical version, and I was excited by the possibilities and challenges. I told Michael that if Pete Townshend was willing to consider getting involved, at least as an advisor and hopefully as an active lyricist-composer, I would be very interested in pursuing it. But I wasn't interested in doing another unofficial version of *Tommy,* which is what the other stage versions that

Choreographer Wayne Cilento and
Des McAnuff in rehearsal, New York,
1993.

I'd heard about seemed to have been. I also knew that we'd have to work hard to adapt *Tommy* to the stage; it wasn't going to be a natural leap, because we were dealing with a song cycle. And in order to maintain the integrity of the piece, I wanted to be able to work with Pete.

Of course, I didn't really expect him to say yes, but I immediately began to prepare. I listened to the original album, and the only decision I made firmly at that point was that I wanted to maintain real respect for the original recording. I wouldn't want to update it or to make it sound like a nineties version. I wanted to capture the sound and spirit of the original and treat it as a classical piece of rock-and-roll, rather than doing what Ken Russell ended up doing with the film, which was to let people bring their own sound to a song— so that Elton John makes "Pinball Wizard" sound like a Bernie Taupin/Elton John song, and Tina Turner makes "Acid Queen" into a Tina Turner song.

That's the only decision I made before meeting Pete. I didn't have something I wanted to present, and I didn't have a pitch or anything remotely like one. I wanted to see what he thought. The only thing I was a little concerned about was that if we were going to do a theatrical version, I didn't think there was time dramatically to fully investigate Tommy's rise and fall at the end. That seemed to me to be a whole other story. On stage you've got the obligation of creating a linear narrative, and you need to explore the episodes in a satisfying way. Things have to move forward in a different way than they do in a song cycle.

I flew over to London in November along with Michael David and Ed Strong from the Dodgers and Gary Gunas and Scott Zeiger from PACE. I was very pleased that I was going to meet Pete—and he didn't disappoint me. He

was very personable and very funny, which was, in a way, what I had expected. There's no question that he's a legend so I couldn't help but be impressed by that, but—he would probably hate my saying this—he's actually rather a warm guy, very good at engaging people and making them feel comfortable.

He and I managed to have this little private conversation in the middle of the larger meeting, while God knows what was being talked about at the other end of the table. But we got about fifteen minutes in and agreed to meet again alone. He was recording the next day, so it had to be the day after that.

The breathing space turned out to be great for me. I was staying at the Portobello Hotel, and I had thirty-six hours before our next meeting. Pete and I had had just enough of a conversation for me to get a sense of what he was concerned about. He wasn't sure whether the musical danced, and that came up strongly in that first meeting. I thought it did, and I felt that the instrumental sections would be very useful as storytelling. He wasn't sure what kind of dance we would apply to that, because, in reality, rock-and-roll really doesn't dance—pop dances. But my notion from the beginning was to use Pete's life as a time line, make the musical a postwar story and use period dance. So we would move from jitterbugging on to rock-and-roll. There's something really odd about those steps danced to that music, and I thought the juxtaposition would create some interesting tension on stage.

With these ideas in my head, I spent thirty-six hours listening to all of the recordings of *Tommy*. I truly basked in the original and also all the cover versions. For thirty-six hours I did nothing but listen. I steeped myself in it, took some notes and came up with a kind of outline to start our conversations with about song order and what the bare bones of the story might be.

It's important to remember that *Tommy* has been lots of things, but it was first and foremost a song cycle, and because it was a song cycle, it didn't have to obey a lot of the conventional narrative and thematic structural rules of drama. It took its own license, and the audience had always been very generous about filling in the gaps. It can be hard for people to forget what they think they now know, because, as I mentioned earlier, Ken Russell did his thing and we all have our own fantasies about what the story is.

But the fact is, on the album, Cousin Kevin and Uncle Ernie were not through-line characters; they were vignettes and cameos. Uncle Ernie reap-

pears for "Holiday Camp," but there's no real story there or, rather, the story is a sketchy series of incidents. And throughout, the time line's rather ambiguous.

So when I sat down, I was trying to create an order of songs that would give us the beginning of the structure for a musical. The other problem that came up as I was listening to it was that I saw it initially as a one-act structure. I couldn't really see how to structure the material to make it into two acts.

Anyway, all I brought into the first creative meeting was notes from having listened for thirty-six hours. That meeting was about five hours long. We just talked and talked and talked and talked about the outline. Pete had a lot of comments, and we switched some things around, and we talked philosophically about the piece.

I think quite quickly in that five hours we also made the biggest decisions— the decision about having more than one Tommy; the critical decision to keep Tommy a local hero for as long as possible, to keep that rise to power very brief; and the decision to create a story about a West London family and to ground it in some way—not to make it a fantasy or go in the direction that I think it's gone in other versions. We didn't approach this idea via theoretical concepts like realism or naturalism—we just knew we wanted to make it a real story for several characters, basically the characters in the family.

By Christmas we'd really made most of our decisions. We'd pitched the song order back and forth by fax, and we didn't make a single change in the libretto during all these meetings to begin with. What we did was tell each other the story, more or less. We would walk through each act, scene by scene, and I would describe some of the visual work that I thought we could do, and Pete would talk about philosophy and then we would discuss themes and characters. We also talked very personally about our experiences as young people growing up—particularly his experiences.

There's been a handy kind of shared history in terms of writing the book together and rediscovering or excavating the story. I think a lot of the events in *Tommy* start with the violence of World War II and whatever values come out of that. Clearly, the trauma that plunges Tommy into his state comes directly from World War II.

Essentially, the pinball machine is really the Stratocaster, or the electric guitar. I didn't really embrace pinball as a metaphor for rock-and-roll until after the opening of the La Jolla production in May 1992, when I recognized that audiences would, of course, buy that as a metaphor—all we had to do was serve it up to them. When Tommy blows up the pinball machine, that's very much, for me, Townshend bashing the guitar.

I think Sally Simpson and what happens to Sally was a kind of tragic and ironic foreshadowing of Cincinnati, and I think Pete thinks so, too. That's another one of the things that makes this story at least somewhat personal for him. That isn't to say that Pete is Tommy, but his life has definitely influenced the story. When we needed a new element so that the Walkers could complete a kind of dramatic arc, it was no coincidence that the new song, "I Believe My Own Eyes," was for two characters who are in their forties. Pete's in his forties now, and he has the wisdom and the maturity to be able to sit down and write that song, which is compositionally very sophisticated. But what I think is really clever about the song is that stylistically he's really captured the original, the way he quotes "Go to the Mirror" partway through it. He doesn't try to make himself twenty-three again, but uses the skills and sophistication he has now as a lyricist-composer in his forties and still manages to evoke the style of the original music. The song is a brilliant achievement.

During this entire project, it was critically important to me not to mess

Ensemble member Paul Dobie and Des McAnuff, New York, 1993.

with *Tommy*, not to turn it into something else but to fulfill it and discover what Pete's original impulses had been, and to respect them—right down to the guitar voicings. I wanted to investigate the work in a serious way, very much the way you would with a classic.

I like to think that the spirit and the basic fabric of the original score is, if not identical, very similar to ours—that ultimately we've used it and have evolved from it, right down to Moon's drumming style. It's obviously not a note-for-note reproduction, and there are changes in terms of the structure of the songs and in some of the lyrics. Of course, it would have been impossible to keep the songs absolutely identical to the original album. The vocal arrangements are now for a company of twenty-six. Plus we're telling a story, and we have the obligations of creating a narrative, so there are internal changes in virtually everything.

Occasionally, of course, we get audience members who resist any changes. There are people who really feel like they own this, that this has been part of them, and they don't want anything to change. They want nothing other than the original album and a concert version by the Who.

But Pete certainly has the right to return to his own work and do what he pleases. It's a sacred right that a writer has. And what I think happens to those folks who are open to *Tommy* is that they get completely caught up in the theatre and the music—they're experiencing a true development and extension of the original album.

—*Interview by Rita D. Jacobs*

SCENE 5: HOSPITAL

—●—

SPARKS (INSTRUMENTAL)

A very concerned Mr. and Mrs. Walker deliver four-year-old Tommy to a young doctor who leads him by hand through a door. The Walkers leave, and during the rest of the scene Tommy is escorted through door after door in a series of examinations and tests. The doctors and nurses usher Tommy around like an automaton. He is the center of a whirl of file cabinets, eye charts and swinging doors as lab technicians work at a counter where tubes are delivered and tested, readings are taken and charts are filled out.

Nurses and doctors hurry about, passing Tommy and clipboards around like batons in a relay race. They check the boy's pulse, reflexes, heartbeat, eyesight and hearing.

In the end, the Walkers return and consult with the young doctor, who shakes his head. For the Walkers this is the real court and the verdict is catastrophic.

As the doctors and nurses walk off with the four-year-old Tommy, a projection tells us it is now 1950, and a nurse enters through another door with the ten-year-old Tommy, who carries a balloon in one hand.

TOMMY BECOMES "DEAF, DUMB AND BLIND" AT A PECULIAR moment in British medical history. In the early forties, medical science was in the midst of what has been a century of exponential growth so rapid that a remove of only a few decades can make an earlier period seem comparably primitive. For example, autism—a mental disorder afflicting young children which Tommy's condition closely resembles—was not given diagnostic criteria until 1943. Tommy's first visit to the doctor might very well have baffled his examiners, since only the most advanced specialist would have the knowledge necessary even to attempt diagnosis of his problem.

Gaining access to such a specialist became considerably easier in the fifties as a result of Britain's massive health-care innovation in socialized medicine, the British National Health Service. State-salaried specialists were no longer confined to the great teaching institutions, and significant barriers such as money ceased to be insurmountable obstacles for people needing specific medical advice—people such as the Walkers.

Unfortunately, support and guidance for parents like the Walkers lagged behind medical advances. Counseling and special peer groups for parents with autistic children, for example, did not begin to emerge until the late sixties. In the interim parents were left to their own resources in dealing with their children's special needs, often with only each other to rely on, a situation which frequently resulted in relationships strained by feelings of guilt and blame.

—Chad Sylvain, Tommy *Dramaturge*

Tommy Deconstructed

To understand the truly traumatic nature of the scene portrayed in "Tommy," and the overwhelming importance of the mirror in the staging of the play, we should look to the work of a French psychoanalyst, Jacques Lacan on "The Mirror Stage" (*Ecrits*, Norton, 1977). Indeed, I wondered whether Pete Townshend and Des McAnuff hadn't in fact been reading Lacan's work as they prepared their script.

The traumatic event—Tommy's loss of sight, hearing and speech—occurs while Tommy gazes at himself in the mirror. According to Lacan, mirror images are involved in the development of a child's sense of self. Without such a sense of self, a child can never learn to say "I" or speak of him or herself as a someone. As parents know, children have a hard time learning how to use the personal pronoun "I". A sense of self has to develop before they are able to do so.

What happens to Tommy's sense of self during the traumatic scene? His self-image—which had originally been positive and coherent—breaks down. His former sense of self shatters when he is confronted with his parents' powerful new view of him as highly dangerous. He is someone who could, with one false move, one inadvertently uttered word, destroy his whole family forever.

Townshend and McAnuff imbue this scene with a momentum unsuspected by those familiar with the record, the volume growing to a moving crescendo as Tommy's biological parents reunite in the urgent attempt to not merely silence Tommy, but to make him block out the whole affair: "You didn't hear it, you didn't see it…" they sing ever more loudly and forcefully. Yet the self known as Tommy did see and hear it and instead of blocking out the incident, he blocks himself out.

Tommy understands that to keep the family together, he must—according to his parents—sacrifice himself. Rather than give up his mother and his new father figure, he prefers to give up his precious seeing, hearing and speaking self. He thus paradoxically chooses to disappear in order to continue to be loved.

—Bruce Fink, Ph.D., from "Rock Musical 'Tommy' Has Resonance in Real Life," *Los Angeles Times,* October 4, 1992

(The Narrator somersaults in from above to join Tommy and his parents on stage.)

AMAZING JOURNEY (REPRISE)

TOMMY   Ten years old
With thoughts as bold as thought can be;
Loving life and becoming wise
In simplicity.

Sickness will surely take the mind
Where minds can't usually go.
Come on the amazing journey
And learn all you should know.

A vague haze of delirium
Seeps in his mind.
Soaring and flying images blind.

I'll be your leader;
I'll be your guide.
On the amazing journey, together we'll ride.

(Unseen by the Walkers, the Narrator takes the balloon from Tommy and floats away with it.)

"The central relationship in the story is between Tommy and Tommy so we created multiple Tommys on stage. Then the concept of the adult reaching the child became very valuable for the first act, and the idea of the child reaching the adult began to function in the second act. In fact, I think those of us who manage to stay spiritually alive have to keep the children in us alive."

—Des McAnuff, *Director*

SCENE 6: CHURCH & THE HOME OF THE RELATIVES, 1950

———●———

(With a giant stained-glass eye projected behind them, the extended family goes to church at Christmas, where the Minister presides over a choir.)

CHRISTMAS

MR. WALKER   Did you ever see the faces of the children?
They get so excited,
Waking up on Christmas morning
Hours before the winter sun's ignited.
They believe in dreams and all they mean,
Including Heaven's generosity.
Peeping 'round the door
To see what parcels are in store,
In curiosity.

MR. & MRS. WALKER
And Tommy doesn't know what day it is.
He doesn't know who Jesus was or what praying is.

ALL   How can he be saved
From the eternal grave?

(The family shakes hands with the Minister and they all proceed to Cousin Kevin's house for Christmas dinner. Ten-year-old Tommy sits rocking on the floor, oblivious to his present, a model of an RAF bomber, which Cousin Kevin opens and plays with for him.)

MR. WALKER   Surrounded by us all, he sits so silently
And unaware of anything.
Playing dumb, he cries, he smiles,
He picks his nose, he pokes his tongue at everything.

THE IDEA OF A CHURCH SCENE AND THE CHRISTMAS DINNER did not exist on the original album. But as the book for the musical was being developed, it became apparent to Pete Townshend and Des McAnuff that there was a thematic thread in the appearance of the institutions of medicine and church—both of which Tommy is taken to for salvation, although ultimately he must find salvation in himself. When medicine fails, the Walkers turn to religion and that is how the minister and his wife came to be characters. Eventually, the song "Christmas" developed into a scene not so much about the holiday as about the way in which formal, organized religion is used in trying to reach Tommy.

"The importance of World War II for this family is undeniable, and the Wellington bomber serves as a symbol for the war through the entire play from the opening scene in the hangar where the Walkers meet. In the Christmas scene the plane appears as a toy, and then again the bomber shows up huge as the back glass to a pinball machine. It becomes a collective image that builds in the audience's mind."

—John Arnone, Set Designer

MINISTER   I believe in love,
But how can men who've never seen
Light be enlightened?
Only if he's cured
Will his spirit's future level ever heighten.

MR. & MRS. WALKER
And Tommy doesn't know what day it is.
He doesn't know who Jesus was or what praying is.

ALL   How can he be saved
From the eternal grave?

(Uncle Ernie plays the French horn to amuse the family; to their amazement, Tommy seems to respond. Mr. Walker notices and crosses to Tommy in amazement.)

MR. WALKER   Tommy, can you hear me?
Tommy, can you hear me?
Tommy, can you hear me?
Tommy, can you hear me?
Tommy, can you hear me?
Can you hear me?

(There is no response from Tommy.)

ALL   How can he be saved?

(Unseen by the others, the older Tommy appears and reaches out to his younger self.)

TOMMY   See me, feel me,
Touch me, heal me.
See me, feel me,
Touch me, heal me.

(The ten-year-old Tommy rises and moves from the table. The Narrator exits as Mr. Walker, noticing that Tommy has moved on his own, goes to him.)

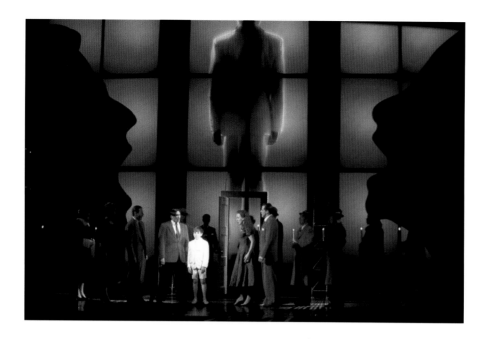

MR. WALKER   Tommy, can you hear me?
                         Tommy, can you hear me?
                         Tommy, can you hear me?
                         Tommy, can you hear me?
                         Tommy, can you hear me?
                         Can you?

MR. & MRS. WALKER
                         Can you…
                         Can you hear me?

ALL   How can he be saved?

(A group of carolers appear at the door, the older members of the family pair off to dance and young Tommy is grabbed by Cousin Kevin and waltzed around the room.)

                         Did you ever see the faces of the children?
                         They get so excited,
                         Waking up on Christmas morning
                         Hours before the winter sun's ignited.
                         They believe in dreams and all they mean,
                         Including heaven's generosity.
                         Peeping round the door
                         To see what parcels are in store,
                         In curiosity.
                         And Tommy doesn't know what day it is.
                         He doesn't know who Jesus was or what praying is.
                         How can he be saved
                         From the eternal grave?

(Uncle Ernie is left on stage alone with a pint of beer in his hand. He downs it in one long gulp. He lets out a thunderous belch and heads for his baby-sitting appointment.)

"The hardest thing about playing Tommy is keeping focused—staring in one place and not moving my eyes around and not talking. Sometimes, it's really hard not to laugh. I just try to think about keeping concentrated, no matter what happens."

—Buddy Smith, *Ten-Year-Old Tommy*

"Sometimes I think about what's going on inside of Tommy's head. I guess, in a way, he can feel all the stuff that's going on in him, and maybe inside he's saying 'Stop' or 'Get me out of here.' He's like a prisoner in his own body."

—Buddy Smith, *Ten-Year-Old Tommy*

———•———

(Uncle Ernie is met at the door by Mrs. Walker, who is getting ready to go out with Mr. Walker for the evening. As Ernie sinks into the sofa, Mrs. Walker anxiously goes on dressing in the bedroom.)

DO YOU THINK IT'S ALRIGHT?

MRS. WALKER   Do you think it's alright
To leave the boy with Uncle Ernie?
Do you think its alright?
He's had a few too many tonight!

MR. WALKER   D'you think it's alright?
I think it's alright.
D'you think it's alright?
Yes, I think it's alright.
Yes, I think it's alright.

(Uncle Ernie sprawls drunkenly on the sofa next to Tommy, who's rocking back and forth. The Walkers kiss Tommy goodnight and walk out the door.)

MRS. WALKER   Do you think it's alright
To leave the boy with Uncle Ernie?
Do you think it's alright?
There's something about this
I don't really like!

MR. WALKER   D'you think it's alright?
I think it's alright.
D'you think it's alright?
Yes, I think it's alright.
Yes, I think it's alright.

MRS. WALKER   Yes, I think it's alright.

(Still sitting on the sofa next to Tommy, Uncle Ernie doesn't touch him, hardly looks at him. He only glances over occasionally to make sure that Tommy can't hear or understand him.)

FIDDLE ABOUT

UNCLE ERNIE   I'm your wicked Uncle Ernie.
I'm glad you won't see or hear me
As I fiddle about,
Fiddle about,
Fiddle about!

Your mother left me here to mind you.
Now I'm doing what I want to…
Fiddling about,
Fiddling about,
Fiddle about!

IN PETE TOWNSHEND'S MIND, THE EVOLUTION OF UNCLE ERNIE is extraordinarily apt. "Uncle Ernie started life as a bad joke. Now he has necessarily become real, believable and unacceptable. Some people in the audience still feel they are expected to laugh when they first see our new (politically correct?) Uncle Ernie sit down beside Tommy. The gross satire produced by Keith Moon and Ken Russell (and which has inspired most celebrity characterizations since) was obviously meant to be surreal; the question now is whether such an approach is acceptable any more. Now so many people have had the courage to come out in public to speak about child abuse, we have to be more direct in our portrayal or symbolism of the abuse itself and perhaps less specific about the emotional and traumatic results. Some people seem to survive cathartically, others by repression and some simply curl up and die.

"What is now certain is that the moment on stage when Tommy gets up from the bed and returns to the mirror, to the safety of his own reflection, we not only have a moving moment, but an elegant truth. This is what I believe happens after experiences like this: until children can articulate what has happened they can only help themselves by creating an alternative reality. It is poignant and tragic at once."

Down with the bedclothes,
Up with the nightshirt!
Fiddle about,
Fiddle about,
Fiddle about!

ENSEMBLE
Fiddle about,
Fiddle about,
Fiddle about!

UNCLE ERNIE You won't shout as I fiddle about.

(Ernie picks Tommy up as though he were a bride and carries him to the bed. Huge projections of open hands fill the background, one after the other.)

UNCLE ERNIE & ENSEMBLE
Fiddle about,
Fiddle about,
Fiddle about!

(He kneels next to Tommy on the bed, which begins to spin demonically.)

Fiddle, fiddle, fiddle,
Fiddle, fiddle, fiddle,
Fiddle, fiddle, fiddle,

Fiddle, fiddle, fiddle,
Fiddle!

(There is the sound of a slamming door and everything stops. The Walkers have come back. Uncle Ernie rushes through the bedroom door, finger to his lips to hush them, and leaves. Tommy crosses into the front room past his parents to stare at himself in the mirror on the wardrobe. The ten-year-old Tommy suddenly sees his older self in the mirror.)

SEE ME, FEEL ME (REPRISE)

(Everything else fades into darkness and all we see is the ten-year-old Tommy gazing at the older Tommy in the wardrobe mirror.)

TOMMY *(to ten-year-old Tommy)*
See me, feel me,
Touch me, heal me.
See me, feel me,
Touch me, heal me.

Creating Uncle Ernie

Ernie has to be played as a very real character because if you make him grotesque, the drama just doesn't work.

He's a man on the outside of everything—and that's how he functions, even in the blocking of the show. He travels around the edge of most things that happen, and has no place to get in. He's not in the army because he's physically impaired by a limp, so he can't take part in that major part of the lives of young men at that time.

In direct contrast to Ernie, his brother, Captain Walker, is a handsome and successful flyer who not only plays a role in the war but has a beautiful wife and can start a family and be loved. He has everything that Ernie lacks, yet Ernie unselfishly adores him.

The moment when the telegram comes to say that Captain Walker is missing is a powerful moment because Ernie loves his brother just as much as Mrs. Walker loves her husband. In my mind, these are two people who love this one other person desperately, and Ernie now feels it's his job to protect his brother's family.

But the thing that makes Ernie most interesting to play is that he is basically a good guy who does a very bad thing, and that's what makes it so affecting. It's also what brings his behavior so close to reality, because a lot of people who do this type of thing are otherwise quite nice people. I take his behavior as a distillation of all of those temptations that we all have—to do something that we know is not only wrong, but that will be hurtful to people or a betrayal of them.

We all come up against an enormous temptation at some time in our lives—a powerful force that drives us towards doing something that we know will be incredibly destructive. And, for just a moment, we feel the pull to do that thing, the lure to do something very terrible, to trespass on a treasured relationship in some way, to cheat in a marriage or betray a close family relationship. If we're honest with ourselves, we can find something like this in our own lives.

That's what Ernie's behavior is about, and that's what "Fiddle About" epitomizes. I hope the fact that we approach him in a very human way makes him an accessible character—because if the audience can understand him as human, then he's truly chilling.

—Paul Kandel, *Uncle Ernie*

John Entwistle   1979

JOHN ENTWISTLE REMEMBERS CREATING COUSIN KEVIN VERY clearly. "Pete asked me to write it because he felt he couldn't write the character as nastily as I could. The idea was to create a bully for a series of traumatic encounters that would rock any senses that Tommy had left. I turned him into a cousin as well.

"As a child I was never the bully—I was one of the bullied. And I actually based Cousin Kevin on a boy who lived across the street. Our parents thought we should play together, and he was completely sadistic. I was much smaller and he played tricks on me and threatened to stick pins in my fingers. But it had a happy ending. I suddenly grew larger and kicked the shit out of him.

"Musically, I wanted the piece to sound both sinister and childish, so I came up with a kind of 'Chopsticks' theme on the piano to make it sound like a simple children's song—but the words he sings are nasty over the top. I got a lot of flak in the sixties about writing such a sick song."

SCENE 8: 22 HEATHFIELD GARDENS

(Tommy is alone at home with Cousin Kevin, his new baby-sitter.)

COUSIN KEVIN

COUSIN KEVIN   We're on our own, cousin.
         All alone, cousin.
         Let's think of a game to play
         Now the grown-ups have all gone away.
         You won't be much fun,
         Being blind, deaf and dumb,
         But I've no one to play with today.
         D'you know how to play hide and seek?
         To find me it would take you a week.
         But tied to a chair you won't go anywhere…
         There's a lot I can do with a freak.

(Cousin Kevin sticks a lampshade on Tommy's head, then flings it away, pushes him out the front door and leaves him out there.)

         How would you feel if I turned on the bath,
         Ducked your head under and started to laugh?
         What would you do if I shut you outside,
         To stand in the rain
         And catch cold so you died?

         I'm the school bully!
         The classroom cheat!
         The nastiest play-friend
         You ever could meet.
         I'll stick pins in your fingers
         And tread on your feet…

(Against a projection of a London back street filled with laundry lines, Cousin Kevin sticks Tommy into the trash can, puts the lid on and sits on top.)

> We're on our own, cousin.
> All alone, cousin.
> Let's think of a game to play
> Now the grown-ups have all gone away.
> You won't be much fun,
> Being blind, deaf and dumb,
> But I've no one to play with today.

(The background changes to the courtyard behind the church. Cousin Kevin rolls the trash can on its side, finally dumping Tommy out in a heap. The Church Youth Club, full of tough-looking boys and girls, gather around them. They toss Tommy around and treat him as if he were a living mannequin, dressing him in odd hats and scarves, sticking cigarettes in his mouth and ears and lighting them.)

COUSIN KEVIN & LOCAL LADS & LASSES

> Maybe a cigarette burn on your arm
> Would change your expression to one of alarm.
> I'll drag you around by a lock of your hair
> Or give you a push at the top of the stairs…
>
> I'm the school bully!
> The classroom cheat!
> The nastiest play-friend
> You ever could meet.
> I'll put glass in your dinner
> And spikes in your seat…

(The Minister and his wife enter and everyone is immediately on their best behavior… until they leave.)

COUSIN KEVIN & LOCAL LADS & LASSES

> We're on our own, cousin.
> All alone, cousin.
> Let's think of a game to play
> Now the grown-ups have all gone away.
> You won't be much fun,
> Being blind, deaf and dumb,
> But I've no one to play with today.

(Bored with Tommy, Cousin Kevin jokingly stands him in front of the Youth Center's pinball machine. Tommy stares into the mirrored surface of the backboard and starts to play. The machine comes to life. The youths gather around him. He plays hypnotically, beating the machine, and begins to rack up an incredible score. Lights flash, bells ring, buzzers sound. The youths start cheering Tommy on as the Narrator tumbles in from above.)

SENSATION

TOMMY

> I overwhelm as I approach you,
> Make your lungs hold breath inside!
> Lovers break caresses for me,
> Love distracted, don't know why.

"When I sing directly to little Tommy, I feel like I'm urging him to follow me as well as trying to communicate compassion. I'm his nurturing, calming inner voice saying 'Trust me, things will be okay, even though they may be hard now. Listen to my voice because I'm you.'"

—Michael Cerveris, Tommy

You'll feel me coming,
A new vibration.
From afar you'll see me.
I'm a sensation…
I'm a sensation!

(The Minister comes back in to see Tommy's miraculous behavior. He leaves quietly shaken.)

TOMMY   They're moved by me and all I touch;
Hazy-eyed, they catch my glance.
Pleasant shudders shake their senses.
My warm momentum throws their stance.

You feel me coming,
A new vibration.
From afar you'll see me.
I'm a sensation…
I'm a sensation!

Soon you'll see me. Can't you feel me?
I'm coming…
Send your troubles dancing. You know the answer:
I'm coming…
I'm coming…
I'm a sensation!

(The youths dance and celebrate wildly as Tommy's pinball score continues to mount.)

TOMMY   I leave a trail of rooted people
Mesmerized by just the sight.
All these lovers feel me coming,
Love as one—in love tonight.

You'll feel me coming,
A new vibration.
From afar you'll see me.
I'm a sensation…

"Cousin Kevin is a lot like the kid who brings the teacher an apple and when the teacher leaves he torments the class. Doing bad things is just his idea of fun, and he sees Tommy as his human rag doll. I sing 'I'll stick pins in your fingers and tread on your toes' to Tommy with the kind of glee you might use saying 'I'll buy you a puppy dog and an ice-cream cone.'"

—Anthony Barrile, *Cousin Kevin*

D R. CLIVE ROBBINS AND DR. PAUL NORDOFF HAVE DEFINED "THE music child" as the part of every human being that can respond to music, despite the limits of any particular disability. Essentially, they believe in the power of music to reach beyond pathology into the healthiest parts of a personality.

In keeping with this theory, music therapists have devised various diagnostic tests to reach nonverbal patients.

Looking for a glimpse into the silent patient's personality, the therapist presents sound stimuli and then records and evaluates whether or not the patient is able to organize a response that recreates the music. In Tommy's case, he imitates the action of striking the cymbal, drum and bell but cannot recreate the rhythm, indicating a profound communication disability.

I'm a sensation!
I'm a sensation…
I'm a sensation!

I am the light.

(The narrator disappears as the Minister brings Tommy's parents in. They stand amazed for a while and then Mrs. Walker puts her arm around Tommy. The Walkers lead Tommy off with renewed hope.)

SCENE 9: A PSYCHIATRIC CLINIC

———•———

SPARKS (REPRISE)

A psychiatrist and his assistant experiment with Tommy. The psychiatrist guides Tommy to a cymbal, a drum and a bell, encouraging him to play each instrument. The Walkers urge Tommy on, but he only responds like a puppet. Mr. and Mrs. Walker become discouraged, Tommy gets very tired and they all seem hopelessly defeated.

SCENE 10: 22 HEATHFIELD GARDENS

———•———

The front door of 22 Heathfield Gardens appears as the disheartened Walkers lead Tommy down the street. Mr. Walker puts his key in the door and lets Mrs. Walker and Tommy enter, while he remains at the doorstep and takes out a package of cigarettes. He is clearly upset.

The Hawker glides down the street, glances through the window and nods at a not yet visible companion. A rather unsavory-looking character, he arrives at Mr. Walker's side in time to light his cigarette. While Mr. Walker smokes, the Hawker begins to sing "Eyesight to the Blind," and pulls out photographs of his woman, which he shows to Mr. Walker. His proposition is clear and Mr. Walker is dubious.

The Hawker's companion appears from down the street, playing wailing riffs on his harmonica. Mr. Walker is now somewhat amused and looks at the photographs again with interest at the prospect of a woman who could cure his son. After some hesitation, he goes inside and rushes Tommy out of the house. Mrs. Walker appears at the door and seems to be about to stop them but then thinks better of it and stands watching them go.

Mr. Walker and Tommy follow the two men through a heavily industrial, urban London landscape. The Hawker continues to sing as he leads them to a godforsaken back alley where aggressive hookers and filthy derelicts crouch around fires burning in oil drums. A group of thugs is gathered around a manhole on a circle of tires while, in the background, drunks sip at cheap beer and rubbing alcohol. Despite the surroundings, Mr. Walker, who is at his wit's end about his son, is eager to meet the woman he's been told has "got the power to heal."

Playing the Lucky Blues

On the day my agent called about *Tommy*, I was delivering pizzas in an old postal jeep I had bought, and feeling frustrated with my career. A friend, who knew I played blues piano, had suggested that since I was spending so much time in the Jeep I ought to do something useful and learn blues harmonica. So I got a couple of harmonicas and would drive with my knee while I taught myself to play. But my mind was really on trying to figure out how to break the cycle of doing regional theater and menial jobs in between.

Then when *Tommy* came up, I knew it didn't make sense to go in and audition with a straight musical number like "Oklahoma!," and I thought, "Now what am I going to do?" It was my wife who said, "You're getting good enough on the harmonica. Just go in and do your thing—sing some blues and play some blues. Show them what you've got and maybe they can use it."

So I walked into the audition and said, "I don't really have anything prepared, but I have a couple of harmonicas—could we jam some blues?" I made up lyrics and played, and Des was just kind of rocking the whole time.

Then I said, "Well, that's about it," and started to walk away. Des stopped me and said, "Wait! Wait a minute! Can you stay for the dance audition?" I said, "Okay," but I was wearing my cowboy boots and didn't have dance shoes with me. I took the boots off and danced barefoot, which I remember very well because my toes were bleeding when we finished. It became kind of a joke—for weeks afterward the cast used to tease me and ask if I could afford shoes yet.

At the end of the audition, when people were leaving, Des came up and said, "That was a lot of fun. You gave me a great idea to try something new." So the Harmonica Player role was created because I walked into the audition and played my heart out. And now I'm getting to do theater and rock-and-roll together on Broadway! It's great—in fact, it's perfect.

—Lee Morgan, *The Harmonica Player*

———●———

(The others slink away as the Hawker and the Harmonica Player lead Tommy and his father to a hooded figure, a drug-addicted prostitute called the Gypsy, badly in need of a fix. She looks down at Tommy, puts her hand on her head and gazes up at the heavens.)

ACID QUEEN

Tina Turner as the Gypsy 1975

WHEN THE ACID QUEEN SINGS HER SONG, PETE Townshend hears the echo not only of his own tenor, but of his own empathy. "This song, written for my own voice, gives me hope that one day I'll be able to write less aggressive and self-destructive songs for women to sing. I've always felt a special chill to hear the great artists who have tackled this. My reading was arch, cold, detached.

"A great female voice, a great woman, can bring to the lyric a sudden glimpse of what it is like to be manipulated by a pimp, or to have to rely on one's own sexual potential to exist, or to feel—ironically—reduced as a human being by one's own beauty."

GYPSY

If your child ain't all he should be now,
This girl will put him right.
I'll show him what he could be now;
Just give me one night.

(The Gypsy removes her cloak and steps into the light.)

I'm the Gypsy—the Acid Queen!
Pay before we start.
I'm the Gypsy—I'm guaranteed
To tear his soul apart.

Give us a room and close the door.
Leave us for a while.
Your boy won't be a boy no more,
Young, but not a child.

I'm the Gypsy—the Acid Queen!
Pay before we start.
I'm the Gypsy—I'm guaranteed
To tear his soul apart.

Gather your wits and hold on fast;
Your mind must learn to roam.
Just as the Gypsy Queen must do,
You're gonna hit the road.

When the work is done, you'll look at him:
He'll never be more alive.
My blood will run through his skin.
Watch his body writhe!

I'm the Gypsy—the Acid Queen!
Pay before we start.
I'm the Gypsy—I'm guaranteed
To tear his soul apart.

(The Gypsy hustles Mr. Walker away from Tommy and over to the Hawker. She dances sinuously around the boy, who seems to respond with a voluntary motion. Mr. Walker is encouraged enough to pay her.)

If your child ain't all he should be now,
This girl will put him right.
I'll show him what he could be now;
Just give me one night.

"The Gypsy's main goal is to get the money so that she can support her habit. But there is a clear and important moment where I feel she realizes she is dealing with a child, and I think there is a part of any woman—I don't care who she is—that is by nature nurturing. Just as she's about to take Tommy away, there's eye contact and an emotional exchange between the Gypsy and Mr. Walker, and she sees a father in the midst of indecision. At that moment she suddenly realizes what she's about to do. This recognition is what humanizes her for me."

—Cheryl Freeman, *The Gypsy*

I'm the Gypsy—the Acid Queen!
Pay before we start.
I'm the Gypsy—I'm guaranteed
To break your little heart.

(The Gypsy starts to lead Tommy off, but Mr. Walker, horrified at the actual deed, changes his mind and pulls him away from her. As they exit, the Hawker takes the money away from the Gypsy, who turns away in despair.)

SCENE 12: AMUSEMENT ARCADE, 1958.

———●———

(A wall of mirrors appears in the background as a slide tells us it is now 1958. A disheveled young Teddy Boy complains to an unimpressed Cousin Kevin, who is filing his nails.)

PINBALL WIZARD

FIRST LOCAL LAD

        Ever since I was a young boy,
        I've played the silver ball.
        From Soho down to Brighton,
        I must have played them all.
        But I ain't seen nothing like him
        In any amusement hall.
        That deaf, dumb and blind kid
        Sure plays a mean pinball!

(A second Teddy Boy stumbles on, clearly another deposed local champion.)

SECOND LOCAL LAD

        He stands like a statue,
        Becomes part of the machine.
        Feeling all the bumpers,
        Always playing clean.
        He plays by intuition;
        The digit counters fall.
        That deaf, dumb and blind kid…

THE TWO LADS

        …Sure plays a mean pinball!

COUSIN KEVIN & THE TWO LADS

        He's a pinball wizard.
        There has to be a twist.
        A pinball wizard,
        S'got such a supple wrist.

FIRST LOCAL LAD

        How do you think he does it?

SECOND LOCAL LAD

        I don't know.

FIRST LOCAL LAD

        What makes him so good?

COUSIN KEVIN   He ain't got no distractions;
        Can't hear those buzzers and bells.
        Don't see no lights a-flashin';
        He plays by sense of smell.
        Always gets a replay,
        'N' never tilts at all.
        That deaf, dumb and blind kid…

IN 1931, DAVID GOTTLIEB MODIFIED AN OLD-WORLD FRENCH GAME, bagatelle, and began to sell his coin-operated game to drugstores and arcades. For a penny, a player could purchase three to four minutes of pinball time.

A few years later more than a hundred companies were producing new versions. Innovations came fast and flashy: the kick-out hole, the tilt mechanism, sounds and lights and thumper bumpers which sent balls zooming around faster and faster.

Pinball's rapid rise was threatened when manufacturers added free game bonuses and even cash payoffs, making pinball seem like a one-arm bandit, without the arm. The game was only saved with the introduction of its hall-mark feature, the flipper, which meta-morphosed pinball from a game of chance to a game of skill.

"In thinking about staging this number, I watched Jailhouse Rock *and other old Elvis Presley movies. In fact, I actually developed some of the dance sequence movements for 'Pinball Wizard' based on a photo of Elvis."*

—Wayne Cilento, *Choreographer*

COUSIN KEVIN & THE TWO LADS
...Sure plays a mean pinball!

(The rest of the arcade assembles around them, complete with funhouse mirrors and several pinball machines played by the local lads and lasses. Cousin Kevin's popularity clearly rests on the unseen Tommy's status as local legend.)

THE TWO LADS
I thought I was
The Bally table king...

LOCAL LADS   ...But I just handed
My pinball crown to him.

LOCAL LASSES   How do you think he does it?

FIRST LOCAL LAD
I don't know.

LOCAL LASSES   What makes him so good?

FIRST LOCAL LAD
Even at my favorite table,
He can beat my best.

SECOND LOCAL LAD
The kids all lead him in
And he just does the rest.

COUSIN KEVIN   He's got crazy flipper fingers;
Never seen him fall.
That deaf, dumb and blind kid...

ALL   ...Sure plays a mean pinball!

(The kids dance around wildly as a teenage Tommy—our Narrator—appears riding in on a pinball machine, to the delight of all the teenagers at the arcade.)

COUSIN KEVIN & LADS
Even at my favorite table,
He can beat my best.
The kids all lead him in
And he just does the rest.
He's got crazy flipper fingers;
Never seen him fall...
That deaf, dumb and blind kid...

ALL   ...Sure plays a mean pinball!!!

(Sirens wail, lights flash, bells ring as Tommy runs up an astronomical score, and the curtain comes down.)

ADOLESCENT CULTURE

Teenage Idyll

Postwar Britain and America witnessed the emergence of a new subspecies of humanity: the teenager. Born in a "boom," raised in peace-time and reaching adolescence in the middle of the affluent society, kids in the fifties had money in their pockets from their part-time jobs in a society that targeted them as spenders. The result was a youthquake.

They had their own music. In England, Tommy Steele became an overnight sensation playing skiffle, and suddenly anyone with a broom-stick, a washboard or just a kazoo could join the fad of do-it-yourself music making. If not skiffle, there was jazz—the people's music where age, race, gender or class did not matter once you walked through the club door. And there was rock-and-roll, the music where age and every-thing else did matter, sometimes violently; primi-tive teenage gangs of the late fifties fought over their turf and their beats.

They had their own clothes. For most of the decade the teen icon of individuality in fash-ion was the new Edwardian, known commonly as the Teddy Boy. "Teddies" wore narrowed trou-sers, brocade waistcoats, turned-up collars and dangling string ties. The Teddy look rescued Edwardian fashion from the thrift-store racks, a regeneration of the recent past as a way of defying participation in the adult future.

They had their own time. Perhaps the essence of being a teenager was simple self-recognition. Parents of fifties teens had spent their own adolescence waiting to become adults. But their children—the Teddies, the rockers, the skiffle players, and the jazz people—were in no hurry to grow up. Adults were square and teen-agers lingered through adolescence exploring their energies and passions, knowing that money in their pockets, the right clothes and the music of choice was all it took to brand oneself a rebel whose cause was youth itself.

—Chad Sylvain, Tommy *Dramaturge*

Townshend Lets Loose

Founding member of the Who and Tommy *composer and lyricist Pete Townshend has, since the Who disbanded, been a solo performer and an editor at Faber and Faber.*

My work constantly readdresses a pivotal moment around which I think most of our lives revolve in this generation. I'm not sure about previous generations, but I think if rock-and-roll is new, and if it's created anything that's new and lasting, it's been the attention to and the importance of that moment: the moment when you are finally liberated from the protection of family, community and society—at your own behest, at your own demand. Suddenly, you are very, very isolated, polarized and, most importantly, incredibly alone, forever.

This is actually what has always happened, in families and in life. As a child—and men are still children when they're seventeen, eighteen, or nineteen years old—you're very much in the protection of the family. You're part of an animal which is comprised of community and family and history and society and future, too.

And then suddenly you're alone. Your rite of passage leads you to aloneness rather than loneliness, and you then devote the rest of your life to finding God, love, and intermeshment with another individual, which you never, ever achieve. You can fuck, you can fight, you can have children, but you're always alone. And what's so brilliant about rock-and-roll is that it's actually the first societally produced manifestation of culture that's actually recognized the importance of this moment.

Tommy is another way of telling that story.

Des McAnuff talks about pinball being a metaphor for rock-and-roll, and I think deaf-, dumb- and blindness is, if you like, a metaphor for that moment of aloneness. The mirror becomes a two-way street—Tommy's going from somewhere to somewhere, and his rite of passage to adulthood is something he passes through and yet can see from both sides. Des staging one boy on one side of the mirror and another on the other made me realize a lot of this.

I now see the entire story of *Tommy* as a metaphor rather than as an allegory. It's a metaphor for loneliness: the loneliness of the teenager who, in the middle of a school playground, surrounded by people playing basketball, is sitting there thinking, "I'm on my own and nobody loves me!" And if you go inside any of those kids, that's what they're all thinking, which is what makes rock-and-roll really striking.

Once Des and I actually came together on that, we were able to allow Tommy to have his teenage years, to have an adolescence where he finds his instrument for expressing himself outside of the family. The early pinball experiences are unwitting; he's unaware of what's going on. He doesn't know

**Pete Townshend performs
with *Tommy* cast members,
China Club, New York, 1993.**

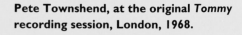

Pete Townshend, at the original *Tommy* recording session, London, 1968.

of the effect that he's having. So when he wakes up, after the mirror smash, he's already on higher ground than he would normally be, because he's already got this local notoriety; he's stunned a few people—he's good at something. It's a kind of innate talent, like kids who have the talent to pop a ball in the basket—those are the kinds of things that actually make you a hero. And this, in combination with the newsworthiness of the cure, the extraordinariness of the cure, conspire temporarily to make him a star—briefly, I feel.

A couple of people have said to me that it all seems to happen so fast, and my feeling is that that's what happens. A story like this, if it were real, would happen very quickly.

There's a moment of tremendous exhilaration when Tommy realizes that he's not only free, but that he can also stop. I think you actually realize the power that Tommy has conferred on himself as a man rather than as a star when he stops the show. It's the power which I had, and I think that that's where we made him real.

What we've actually done is we've closed the loop, definitely, on the original intention of the piece, which was to make a comment about what happens to you spiritually when you finally decide to turn to God or to the inner life, or whatever it is; that the contract that you make, the surrender that you make, is internal, absolute, and you can't go back on it, and once you're on that road, you can never turn back. And now, my feeling is that that kind of allegorical idea actually has a much more satisfying and appropriate reading in the show, because it's become a metaphor for that teenage moment. So his heroism is brief, but real. It's interrupted by the accident at the performance when he pushes Sally off the stage.

In this piece Tommy takes responsibility for throwing Sally off the stage. I think that this was something that we actually had to confront, that we couldn't leave open, as it had been on the original record. My idea was always that Tommy was innocent but culpable, if that's not a contradiction. He was responsible, but the machine of merchandising, spiritual merchandising, TV evangelism that grew up around him was useful to him. It was an echo of what had happened to him when he was a kid and first played pinball.

As something of an incisive aside, what's very perverse is that we now see in the story that Tommy needs Cousin Kevin, who was a bully—he needs

Pete Townshend in Ken Russell's movie *Tommy*, 1975.

The Who in concert: *(left to right)*
Roger Daltrey, Keith Moon,
John Entwistle, Pete Townshend.

his approval, and that's kind of weird. What happened to me in my life was that for a long time I would actually hang on to the people that bullied me a lot when I was young. I wouldn't let them go. And for a long time I thought it was because, in some way, I needed to stay in their orbit so that I could at some point see the fact that they were impressed with who I'd become. But I think it's actually about vengeance; I think it's about keeping hold of those people so that you can torture them. In the show, Kevin eventually addresses Tommy as "Sir."

What is actually depicted in the Sally's-question scene is a timeless debate—when somebody says, "Oh, so and so's great," there will always be somebody else asking,"Why?" But it hasn't occurred to Tommy that people were not finished debating whether or not he's genuine, or whether or not he's real, or whether or not he's just been a con trick. They don't know if he was deaf, dumb and blind or if he was pretending.

When Sally hits him with a real left-field question, he's as confused as she is. He doesn't know what the fuck she's talking about: "What music? This is not what this is about. You don't understand. I'm just normal and I'm having a good time, and isn't that what we're all doing? We're all here to have tea." And she's saying, "No, there's more."

I think she's asking a very sincere spiritual question. She's asking him to give her something special because she's been beaten up—she says "Pay me back; give me something." He could have just picked up a piece of paper and said, "That's it; read it later," and she would have been completely happy. But what he doesn't do is he doesn't attend to that at all. He doesn't attend to her individual need. He's actually very cold with her. And he keeps her at a distance

because at this point he still has much bigger work to do with his family.

Sally's offering everything. She's asking the question, and also saying, "You beat me up; I'm still here. I'll do anything. I'm yours." And so there's a generosity to it on her part, which I don't think is either uniquely feminine or uniquely groupie, but she's actually offering herself. He's just not hip to it.

The immortalization of the audience member and the groupie in one character was a need of mine in this new reading of Sally Simpson. I wanted her to be all those kids that died at Cincinnati, all of those kids that got pushed around at various gigs and, also, all of those people who very, very sincerely want to get something from their heroes which maybe their heroes are incapable of giving.

What's interesting is that the Sally Simpson moment now in the show is one of the great moments. Des and I realized that we had a song here that really works as a dramatic pivot: she becomes the reason why Tommy stops. Not just because she gets beaten up, but also because she asks him a question that he doesn't answer satisfactorily. It's as though somebody said to me, "It must be wonderful being famous," and I responded, "Well, it's just a fucking show, or it's just rock-and-roll," or whatever it is that I might say. It's not the right answer. "It's only rock-and-roll" is not the right answer.

The motivation for the press and the acolytes turning around and saying "We're not gonna take it!" is Tommy's treatment of Sally. They feel that he owes her something, and they're right! I've been through Cincinnati and endless depositions, with lawyers sitting across from me looking at me like I'm the archdevil of rock-and-roll. All the while I would be trying to find some way to say, "Well, you know, this wasn't my fault." But in the end, I realize that

Pete Townshend with musical director Joe Church and Jeanine Levenson, New York, 1993.

whether it's my fault or not, I happen to be the person who's central to the issue.

That moment with Sally has been very, very difficult to bring properly to life in perspective, because firstly, it was a precognizance—I wrote *Tommy* before Altamont. So I hadn't heard of all the kids that had actually died at concerts, but I had seen rough stuff. We'd had incidents at our concerts, and so had lots of other performers. I think this moment in the show is crucial. It's society saying, "This isn't good enough. Somebody has got to be responsible"—and that person has got to be the figurehead. If you're the figurehead for the success, you've got to be the figurehead for the failure, too.

This part of *Tommy* is, too, a study of celebrity. The people who reject Tommy say if you're going to behave like this, you're not a hero anymore, because you're just normal. We're telling you we've elected you as a star. We've made you famous; we're here to take your picture; we're here to interview you. You're saying that you want to be like us? Come and work twelve hours a day for a newspaper! Come and do what I do, cleaning the roads. There's a naiveté and innocence in Tommy that really amounts to ignorance and unfeelingness. He's a dumb kid who hasn't lived, and that's what they're reacting against.

In the show Tommy becomes a symbol for everything. And the audience is invited to join in when he's being disposed of. What we're doing there is saying that he's not playing the game. And that actually becomes an extraordinarily profound moment for me, because I really do think that life, not just show business, is about submission. I think that living is about submission. I think that in order to live on a planet with billions of other people, you have to learn to submit; you have to learn a kind of unwilling, uncomfortable selflessness. He refuses to compromise—not out of bullishness, but out of innocence. He's stupid. All he has to do is to say to Sally, "Oh, but you can be like me. Hang out for a while. Let's smoke a joint. Let's have a beer." But he actually says, "You fools! How can you be like me? I had a terrible time."

What's quite interesting about the icon/heroism of rock-and-roll in the sixties and seventies is that it was rooted in the idea that people who were performers would necessarily get the good word first—the idea that if the Maharishi was a smart guy, that the Beatles would find him first. Therefore that should be good enough for the rest of us. And to some extent Sally is saying,

"You're there, you're on the case, you know what's happening; tell me what's happening." But what she's really saying is, "Fuck me, I'm here for you, on your terms. You define the terms." What he's saying back is, "You don't understand." And it's quite clear that he doesn't understand, that at that point he's the ingenue. He's the neophyte. He's the guy who really doesn't know what's happening, because when he goes back to his family, the first thing he's got to do, presumably, is get out there and get laid. That's where *Tommy* ends.

People ask me whether there is a truth in the story of Tommy. But truth is finite. There are aspects of truth, or moments of truth, or fragments and slivers of truth—only what any one man or writer or artist can actually handle. The whole truth is a pretty tall order.

But I think that there's a real lesson in *Tommy*. There's a conclusion now. It's almost kind of blasphemous to say this, because my rock-and-roll training is so absolutely antithetical to this. What you don't do in a rock song is you don't draw a conclusion. You offer an idea, you offer a pathway, you offer to share a frustration or an aspiration. But then you don't say, "And the way that we achieve this, or the way that we answer this, is by doing this." But there is a conclusion in *Tommy*.

And the ending dates back to the beginning— to my first meeting with Des. I said, "What's different about this time, Des, when we address *Tommy*, is that I know how the story ends, and I know why the story is, and I know the degree to which the story is autobiographical and the degree to which it isn't autobiographical." This incarnation of *Tommy* has completely changed my work and my life.

—*Interview by Rita D. Jacobs*

Michael Wilson, Lisa Mordente, Wayne Cilento, McAnuff, Lisa Portes and Townshend in rehearsal, New York, 1993.

ACT 2

THE YEAR IS 1960. TOMMY HAS BECOME THE PINBALL CHAMPION AND hero of the neighborhood lads. Mr. Walker, still in search of a cure, convinces Mrs. Walker to try once more, and they take Tommy to high- tech medical specialists for elaborate tests, but to no avail.

Later, on the street, a group of teenaged louts surround Tommy and carry him home, where the Walkers, at their wits' end, compassionately confront one another about what is to be done with their son. Tommy stares into the mirror as Mrs. Walker tries desperately to reach him. Frustrated, she smashes the mirror into which he continually stares. With the mirror shattered, Tommy becomes conscious, announces his freedom, rejects his family and leaves home. His "miracle cure" hits the news.

From 1961 to 1963 Tommy is lionized by the public and the press and begins appearing in stadiums, where Uncle Ernie tries to capitalize on his stardom. At one of the concerts his teenaged fan Sally Simpson manages to get on stage and touch Tommy, but when he pushes her aside, she falls and is pummeled by the guards. Aghast, Tommy realizes how caught up in the celebrity machine he has become. He tends to her and invites everyone back to his house. Once there, in front of the gathering crowd, Sally asks Tommy how she can be more like him. Rather naively, he insists there is no reason to be like him—who she is is enough.

Disenchanted with their hero for failing to provide salvation, the crowd, refusing to accept his answer, turns on him and leaves. After they've departed, Tommy, left alone with only his family, hears the voice of his ten-year-old self and, for a moment, seems to be reverting to his old state. But instead, he turns to his family and embraces them in acceptance and understanding. The amazing journey is now complete.

UNDERTURE

1960: *In the arcade, against a background of brilliantly colored pinball images, Tommy is playing at a pinball machine, surrrounded by the youths. Tommy, at twenty, is a neighborhood celebrity and the adored official mascot of this particular local gang. His playing builds to a fever pitch; a buzzer sounds as he beats the machine. The lads scream in victory…*

LOCAL LADS
Right!!!

…and carry Tommy over their heads down the street, with Cousin Kevin leading the way.

LOCAL LADS
Oy! Oy! Oy! Oy! Oy! Oy! Oy!…

SCENE 13: THE SUNLIGHT LAUNDRETTE

———•———

(The local lads carry the inert Tommy into the Sunlight Laundrette where Mrs. Walker, quietly folding her laundry, watches their loutish but lively behavior with some sadness. They deposit Tommy on a chair and depart.)

IT'S A BOY (REPRISE)

MRS. WALKER   Hmm Hmm Hmm,
        It's a boy, Mrs. Walker, it's a boy.
        It's a boy, Mrs. Walker…

(She crosses to Tommy and gently wipes something from his face with a tea towel. Mr. Walker rushes in, bursting with his news.)

THERE'S A DOCTOR

MR. WALKER   There's a man I've found
        Could bring us all joy!
        There's a doctor I've found can cure the boy!
        A doctor I've found can cure the boy!

MRS. WALKER *(cynically)*
        A doctor you've found can cure the boy!

MR. WALKER   There's a man I've found can remove his sorrow.
        He lives in this town. Let's see him tomorrow.

MR. & MRS. WALKER
        Let's see him tomorrow!

(The Walkers lead Tommy out of the laundrette and into a very modern laboratory.)

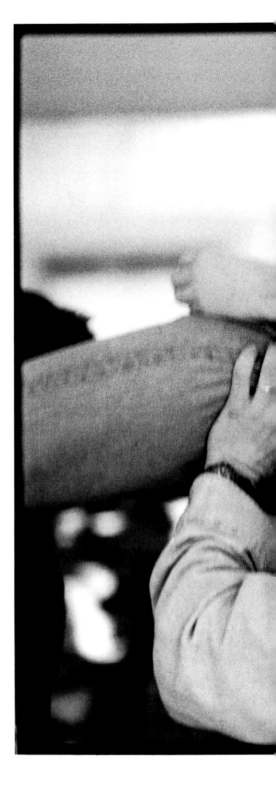

"Some actors might feel naked without words, but I've always loved parts where you're on stage for a while before you have to speak. You get to be at home physically in the space and get comfortable in front of the audience before you have to project your character verbally."

—Michael Cerveris, Tommy

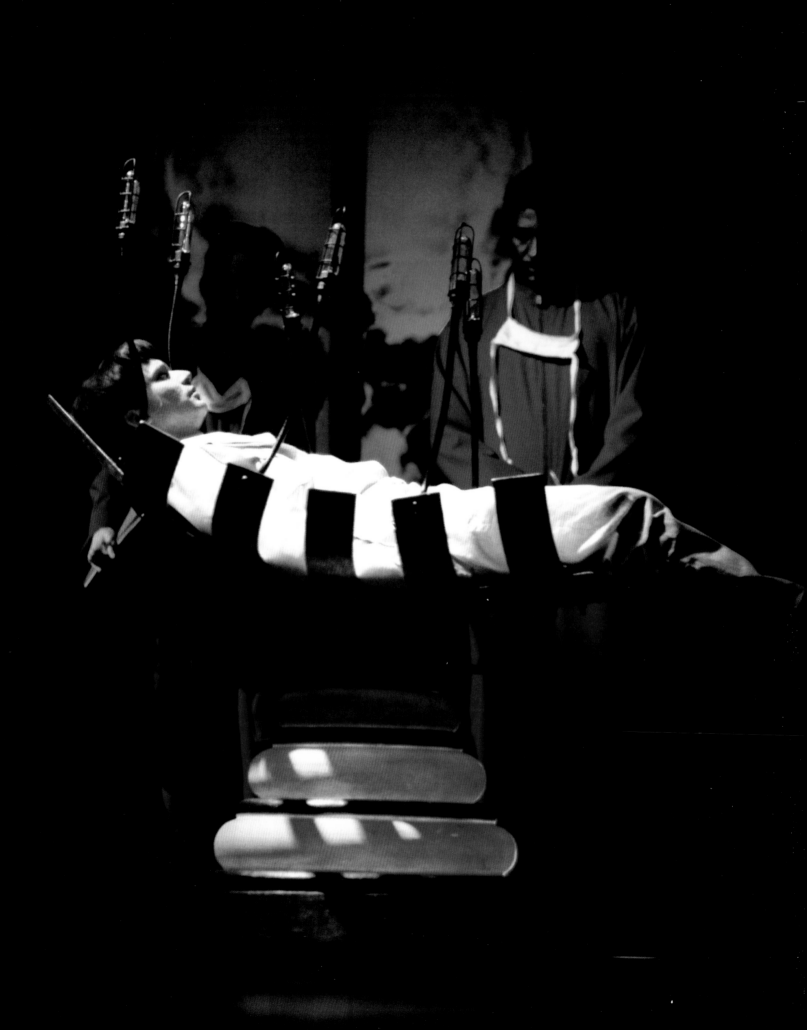

SCENE 14: A RESEARCH LABORATORY

———————●———————

(The modern research laboratory is teeming with lab technicians, as the Specialist speaks to the Walkers about Tommy's condition.)

GO TO THE MIRROR

SPECIALIST He seems to be completely unreceptive.
The tests I give him make no sense at all.

SPECIALIST & SPECIALIST'S ASSISTANT
His eyes react to light; the dials detect it.
He hears but cannot answer to your call.

(Against a background of atomic images and X-rays, Tommy is placed in a nightmarish contraption that spins around 360 degrees.)

TEN-YEAR-OLD TOMMY *(voice-over)*
See me, feel me,
Touch me, heal me.
See me, feel me,
Touch me, heal me.

SPECIALIST There is no chance; no untried operation.
All hope lies with him and none with me.
Imagine, though, the shock from isolation
If he suddenly could hear and speak and see.

(Tommy is moved onto a glowing, brightly colored table that slides him into the tunnel of a similarly brilliant CAT-scan machine. Multiple images of the brilliant readings of the machine appear on the screens behind them.)

TEN-YEAR-OLD TOMMY *(voice-over)*
See me, feel me,
Touch me, heal me.
See me, feel me,
Touch me, heal me.

SPECIALIST His eyes can see,
His ears can hear, his lips can speak.
All the time the needles flick and rock.

SPECIALIST & SPECIALIST'S ASSISTANT
No machine can give the kind of stimulation
Needed to remove his inner block.

Go to the mirror, boy!
Go to the mirror, boy!

(The Specialist turns Tommy toward the mirror; he walks to it and stares at his own image.)

MRS. WALKER I often wonder what he's feeling.
Has he ever heard a word I've said?

"Lighting evokes different emotions and states of mind, and in creating the lighting for Tommy's world I tried to underscore his traumatic state through the use of color. His interior world was filled with heavy, unreal colors so I often used strong, saturated color combinations."

—Chris Parry, Lighting Designer

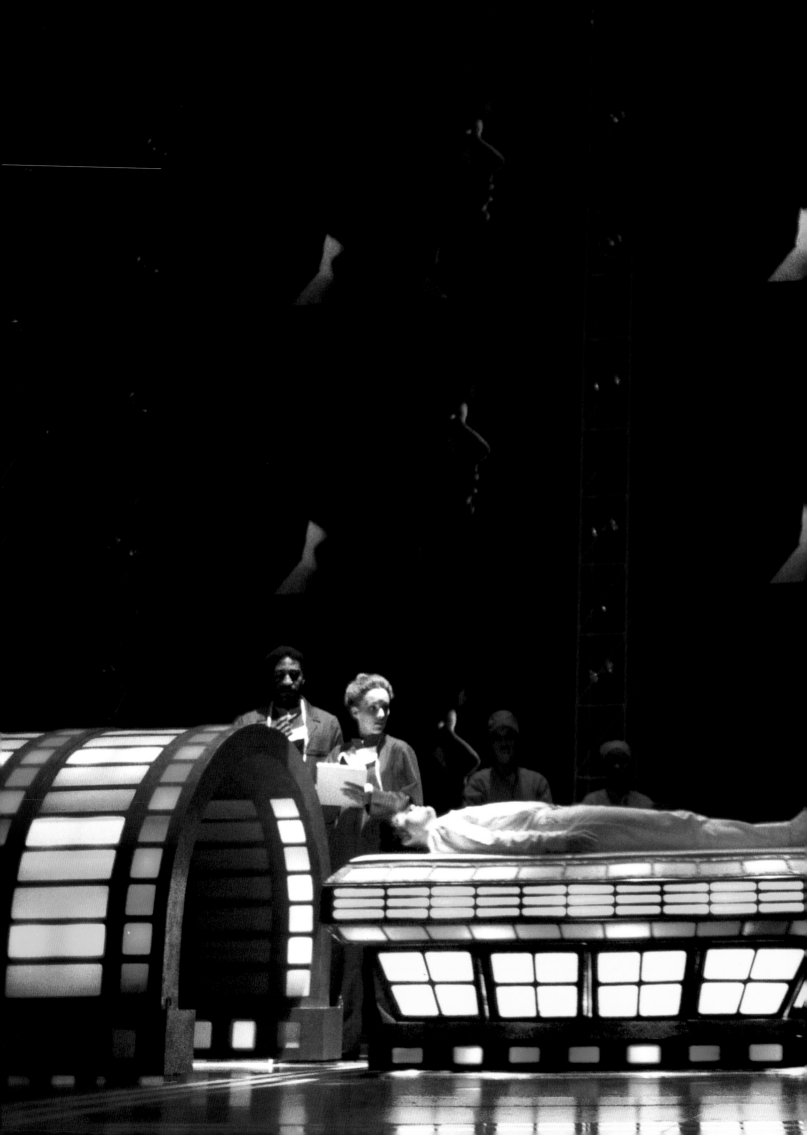

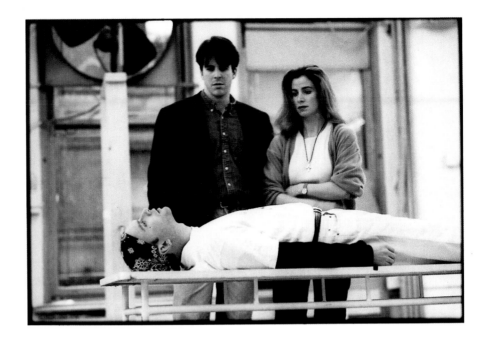

MR. & MRS. WALKER

> Look at him in the mirror, dreaming.
> What is happening in his head?

(Tommy sees his four-year-old and ten-year-old selves in the mirror.)

THE TWO YOUNG TOMMYS

> Listening to you, I get the music;
> Gazing at you, I get the heat.
> Following you, I climb the mountain.
> I get excitement at your feet!

(As Tommy joins in the singing, he levitates several feet off the floor, unnoticed by anyone.)

THE THREE TOMMYS

> Right behind you, I see the millions;
> On you, I see the glory.
> From you, I get opinions;
> From you, I get the story.

(Tommy lands gently back on the floor as his younger selves disappear.)

MR. & MRS WALKER

> What is happening in his head?
> Oooh, I wish I knew…
> I wish I knew.

(Left alone on stage, Tommy is beginning to surface into consciousness. Very slowly, he raises his hand and stares at it.)

"We structured the episodes as an alternating series of abuses and treatments. The sci-fi CAT scan is the last step in the search for a cure."

—Des McAnuff, Director

SCENE 15: THE STREET/22 HEATHFIELD GARDENS

———•———

(Projected scenes of urban industry give way to a tough-looking street where Cousin Kevin joins some leather-jacketed rockers surrounding Tommy.)

COUSIN KEVIN *(spoken)*
Tommy's been to hospital.

FIRST LAD
Oh, he's been cured then, has he?

COUSIN KEVIN
Oh, completely cured, yeah. He's a wonder of science.
They're going to make him prime-fucking-minister.

TOMMY CAN YOU HEAR ME?

(The lads start playing roughly but good-naturedly with Tommy. 22 Heathfield Gardens assembles behind them.)

LOCAL LADS   Tommy, can you hear me?
               Can you feel me near you?
               Tommy, can you see me?
               Can I help to cheer you?
               Oooh, Tommy, Tommy, Tommy, Tommy…

(Cousin Kevin knocks on the Walkers' door and the youths carry Tommy into the house and deposit him on the sofa.)

LOCAL LADS   Tommy, can you hear me?
               Can you feel me near you?
               Tommy, can you see me?
               Can I help to cheer you?
               Oooh, Tommy, Tommy, Tommy Tommy.
               Tommy, Tommy, Tommy…

(The lads file out, one giving Mrs. Walker a flower from her own vase. The image of Tommy as a ten-year-old magically appears in the mirror.)

TEN-YEAR-OLD TOMMY
               Tommy, Tommy, Tommy, Tommy, Tommy.

(Tommy crosses to the mirror and stares. Mr. Walker stiffens.)

"I developed a signature movement, a kind of physical vocabulary, for the louts, with their heads bobbing and their characteristic little jumps. And if you follow the louts through the show, you can see the development of these movements, starting with 'Sensation.'"

—Wayne Cilento, Choreographer

SCENE 16: 22 HEATHFIELD GARDENS

———————•———————

(Oblivious to the young Tommy in the mirror, the Walkers sit at the table. Mrs. Walker shuffles a deck of cards.)

MRS. WALKER *(spoken, to Mr. Walker)*
Like to play, love?…

(Silently fuming, Mr. Walker doesn't respond.)

MRS. WALKER
Suit yourself.

I BELIEVE MY OWN EYES

MR. WALKER   This can't continue.
It makes no sense.
We're getting nowhere.
I've lost all my confidence.
The boy wants something,
I'm satisfied;
He needs attention
And care our love can't provide.
And then, there's the matter of us…

(Mr. Walker takes his wife's hands and holds them with tender intensity.)

I'd like to prove
That I don't think that you've
Seen the best of me.
I've stood up for the boy
And I've clung to the hopes and the lies.
I wish that the pain
In your gaze could again
Be a test of me,
But when I look in the mirror
I believe my own eyes.

(Mr. Walker crosses to Tommy, still staring into the mirror.)

I believe my own eyes,
Know I've come to the end:
All my patience is gone.
When I'm doubtful, I tend
To believe my own eyes.

MRS. WALKER   I'd like to declare
This devotion and care
Is the life to live.
That nothing has changed
And that time isn't passing us by.
But I have to say here
That, for us, there's a clear-
Cut alternative.

THE NEW SONG PETE TOWN-SHEND WROTE FOR *TOMMY*, "I Believe My Own Eyes," surprised even him. "The song turns out to be a conventional music-theatre number in many respects. This is because it performs a conventional function. It has a job to do. It has to suggest the passing of time and patience and must strengthen the audience's feeling that the parents are exhausted but still young enough at heart to hope for their relationship. It also must keep the audience's focus on the mirror, about to be smashed by the mother. And it has to attend to the idea that when there are no answers we have to look inside.

"There was one other, less specific, part of the brief—and that was that we wanted a ballad, something like 'Behind Blue Eyes' from the Who. I trawled all these elements together and came up with the song. By doing so, I surprised myself and everyone else. It is not as popular a song in the show as I had hoped, but it is vital and it works. It is the one piece of new writing I have done for the show that makes me feel I can really write music drama in the future."

When we look at each other
We believe our own eyes.

(Mrs. Walker leads Tommy gently to the sofa and sits him down.)

MR. & MRS WALKER

I believe my own eyes,
Know I've come to the end:
All my patience is gone.
When I'm doubtful, I tend
To believe my own eyes.

This has gone far enough!
After all we've been through…
We can't be blamed;
We've done all we can humanly do.
It's a time to be tough,
A time to be wise.
We must stop chasing false dreams
And recover our lives.

(The Walkers face each other and themselves in the mirror.)

I believe my own eyes,
Know I've come to the end:
All my patience is gone.
When I'm doubtful, I tend
To believe…

I'd like to believe
That I don't feel we've
Seen the best of us.
And the way to believe
Is to see where the real future lies.
I hope that the pain
In your gaze can again
Be the test of us.

And when I look in the mirror
I believe my own eyes.

Let's believe our own eyes.
Know we've come to the end:
All our patience is gone.
Let's admit we intend…

MR. WALKER *(exiting)*

…To believe our own eyes.

MRS. WALKER   …To believe our own eyes.

(The image of Tommy as a four-year-old appears in the mirror.)

"One of the interesting things for me about the Walkers is the difference between them: she seems to be able to accept Tommy's condition in a way that Mr. Walker just doesn't seem capable of. He's the one who's always trying really desperately for the cure in 'There's a Doctor,' 'Acid Queen,' and so on. And it's actually Mr. Walker who eventually starts to turn his back on the kid. He kicks off 'I Believe My Own Eyes.'"

—Des McAnuff, Director

FOUR-YEAR-OLD TOMMY
Tommy, Tommy, Tommy, Tommy, Tommy.

(Tommy crosses to the mirror and stares. Furiously, Mrs. Walker wrenches him away from his reflection.)

SMASH THE MIRROR

MRS. WALKER   You don't answer my call
With even a nod or a wink
But you gaze at your own reflection!
You don't seem to see me
But I think you can see yourself.
How can the mirror affect you?

Can you hear me
Or do I surmise
That you fear me?
Can you feel my temper
Rise, rise, rise, rise,
Rise, rise, rise, rise,
Rise, rise, rise, rise,
Rise!

Do you hear or fear or
Do I smash the mirror?
Do you hear or fear or
Do I smash the mirror?

(Mrs. Walker tries to pull Tommy away from the mirror, but each time one of the younger Tommys appears in the mirror, Tommy tries to move toward the image of the child.)

DESPITE A BURGEONING AWARENESS OF FEMALE individuality and sexuality marked by the publication of the Kinsey report *Sexual Behavior in the Human Female,* the real emphasis on women's roles in the 1950s was rooted in the more traditional realm of domesticity. In fact, the image of woman as wife and mother reached its twentieth-century apotheosis in postwar society.

Doctors Bowlby and Spock were the gurus of motherhood. Bowlby elevated mother love to the point where its deprivation could even account for physical conditions such as stunted growth. Spock relegated rigid rearing practices to the background, advocating "natural loving" and trust to common sense and instinct.

At home women were liberated in the new, servantless society by an onslaught of technological assistance, such as refrigerators, pop-up toasters, washing machines, and vacuum cleaners. Getting out of the home was a matter of hopping into a newly acquired automobile, sometimes to head for work; one in three women in postwar Britain held a job. Women suddenly had their own money and more time to spend it.

But abundance had its negative side—with so much material, technological and informational assistance at hand, women seemed to be the only focus for domestic problems. Blame for the Walkers' troubled home would fall acutely on Mrs. Walker. With so much advice and so many choices, how else could one explain such an obvious failure but to say that somewhere along the way Mrs. Walker had taken the wrong advice or made the wrong choice?

—Chad Sylvain, Tommy *Dramaturge*

MRS. WALKER   Do you hear or fear or
                        Do I smash the mirror?

(Mrs. Walker picks up a chair and threatens to smash the mirror with it.)

MRS. WALKER   Do you hear or fear or
                        Do I smash the mirror?

(In the mirror appears the image of the terrified four-year-old Tommy from the night of the killing long ago. Mrs. Walker furiously swings back the chair…)

(Everything goes black. In the darkness we hear the crash of breaking glass and the sound of a gunshot. In the background are projections of a shattered house and the Lover falling dead. The mirror has been completely smashed. Tommy looks around and sees everything in the room. He stands in the spot where the Lover was killed and kneels to touch the floor. He looks at his mother and reaches out to touch her. She embraces him, but he does not reciprocate. She rushes off to get Mr. Walker.)

"I've spent so much time sitting with my eyes unfocused in an empty state that during the blackout after the mirror is smashed I have to prepare myself to function again. It's a bit like waking up in the morning and alerting your limbs that they're going to have to start working. But of course, for Tommy, this is a profound waking up into a state of innocent wonder at everything around him."

—Michael Cerveris, Tommy

I'M FREE

TOMMY   I'm free... I'm free...
                    And freedom tastes of reality.
                    I'm free... I'm free...
                    And freedom lies here in normality.

(Mrs. Walker returns with Mr. Walker and they watch Tommy in utter amazement.)

                    I could tell you what it takes
                    To feel the highest high.
                    You'd laugh and say "Nothing's that simple!"
                    But you've been down this path before
                    While I was waiting at the door.
                    This place is sacred as a temple.

(Uncle Ernie enters and Tommy's family gathers to watch him in amazement.)

TOMMY   I'm free... I'm free.
                    Right here I've found immortality!

(The Minister knocks on the door and is dragged in to witness Tommy's miraculous change. Uncle Ernie takes Tommy's photograph.)

TOMMY   I'm free... I'm free.
                    And freedom tastes of reality!

(Mr. Walker opens his arms to embrace his son, but Tommy sharply pushes him away. Tommy opens the front door and walks down the street, looking at all that surrounds him.)

"In a way, your house offers protection—the windows and doors provide a shelter for your personality or identity as it relates to your parents. Within those confines, you don't have to risk much, but once you step outside, like Tommy, you have to deal with the world."

—John Arnone, Set Designer

Tommy Rocks Broadway

Matt Resnicoff

At the time *Tommy* began previews on Broadway in March 1993, Richard Strauss' *Ariadne auf Naxos* was finishing a run uptown at the Metropolitan Opera House, the same New York hall where the Who, in 1970, first performed their rock opera in its entirety—heretically, many felt, for the location. Ariadne is one of opera's great lost souls, spurned by Theseus after giving him the string that led him out of the labyrinth. Her story played at the Met in lustrous grandeur; she is deceived, she is consoled, she is exalted.

As outraged as opera might have been at the intrusion of rock in her salon—its daring to "rock her world," as they say—she must have had an easier time adjusting to the Who than Broadway did in 1993. What Tommy shares with Ariadne, besides his divine sensibility (*Ariadne*'s last line: "When a new god comes along, we're dumbstruck") is a complex tale told through song, with updated staging and an almost sacrosanct, mythical score. In musical theatre or opera the music can function almost narratively, capable of offering its own wry or sprightly or foreboding commentary, with the baton dictating the rhythm. Passages may lapse into slightly freer imprecision, or a tympani might make what sounds like an errant suggestion about the drama, but the baton is god, always and forever. Rock-and-roll, by strident contrast, rings the toll of the almighty drum and guitar, patently defined by the styles of Keith Moon and Pete Townshend. The Who didn't simply perform *Tommy*, they cauterized it.

In theatre and in opera the performers carry more of the burden than the material (as *Tommy*'s author maintained, it's the *singer*, not the song). *Tommy* on Broadway confounds the traditions of the market; it became a major draw stacked with unknowns. The play's power may simply be the familiarity of its musical themes, but it's still worth looking at how a work so associated with a rock group's endemic ferocity could be so easily disassociable from its source—and how a piece so experimental, so spiritual, so deliciously Freudian could have popular success on Broadway. One perilous hurdle in stage adaptation is that instrumental music usually becomes incidental music, a backdrop to a plot; onstage with the Who, *Tommy*'s story almost seemed an excuse for the music. Broadway's more earthbound version of their transcendental "Sparks" is heard, of all places, during a doctor's appointment. In one sense this transplant deprives the listener of a chance to be taken aloft, to experience the character's detachment and his liberation.

Townshend agrees with this charge, but warns against being too parochial about rock. "The two things exist side by side," he says. "You can't reinvent rock-and-roll for Broadway. It's a different thing. And the theatre does have this difficulty, which is that you have to close the loop—*something* has to be happening on the stage," he laughs, "and somebody has to decide what it is."

The most dramatic changes to *Tommy*'s music, therefore, *are* the dramatic changes, those necessary to accommodate the rigors of dance, or

Right: Pete Townshend in concert, mid-1970s.

Below: String players, *Tommy* orchestra, New York, 1993.

117

support what were once tenuous lyrical connections between scenes. Wartime images extend into ethereal piano interpretations of the "It's a Boy" theme, while "Amazing Journey" is paced faster to underscore the confusion surrounding Tommy's trauma, a modification which is meant to take our minds, entrenched as they are in media-dependent Americana, where "moynds cawn't usually go." Spaces between songs like "Smash the Mirror" and "I'm Free" contain subtle implications of those tunes or themes about to be introduced. Like the new visual of young Tommy facing the mirror and singing his own name as a mantra, the changes want to act as a guidepost to the individualism embedded in the original work. In the smash of the mirror, which cures him, we see on projection screens the murder of his mother's lover—an apparition of the same violence which shut him down in the first place. The story of *Tommy* the album is, in another sense, restored by *Tommy* the musical.

Who drummer Keith Moon.

But something else happens to music when its distinguishing features are scrutinized and regrafted onto a resurrected body: it becomes colloquial. Within rock's first rush of serious innovation, which I'd estimate as a sustained period between 1969 and 1977, the Who could perform most of Townshend's demanding material as a three-piece with vocals, asking only that their audience accept his occasional backing tape as a luxury of embellishment. They aren't remembered as one of the period's best bands for their faithful attention to their guitarist's material or arrangements, or for participating in the sort of misguided anarchism which often passes for "great rock performance." Townshend, Moon, Entwistle and Daltrey landed somewhere squarely in the middle—their interaction as a stretching, improvising unit ignited their treatment of song, but also allowed them the freedom to tear those forms apart and extrapolate on the themes. To convey strong conceptual motifs like those in *Tommy*, they could rely on vignette and allusion, and make up the difference by intensifying the aural experience. The Who transformed into something approaching a jazz band with a bunch of cogent stories to tell; if they played the same song the same way on two consecutive evenings, they simply weren't cutting it. By rejecting the superficial conventions of their medium and taking what amounted to a nightly leap of faith that they'd succeed, they became Tommy—hopelessly imperfect, delightfully unhinged.

The music of *Tommy* the musical is being performed eight times a week with exacting precision, deep within the bowels of Manhattan's St. James Theatre: Imagine a throng of working musicians occupying a space barely large enough to accommodate their instruments alone. In the mouth of this dark steel cage, inches from the cuffs of first-row theatregoers, music director Joe Church stands surrounded by video monitors and cameras linked to stagehands who take cues from the pacing of his baton; an assortment of chairs, music stands and keyboards obstructs any likely passage or possibility of comfort. With every wire-strewn inch of pit floor filled, *Tommy*'s string quartet squeezes into the only other vacant location in the building, a small unused dressing room—on the seventh floor, wired into the conductor's video surveillance system.

The plan was to make *Tommy* authentic but not nostalgic, though no measure of technology alone could ensure that leap of intent. Church sat with choreographer Wayne Cilento and director Des McAnuff and analyzed the Who's original recording, for which McAnuff and Pete Townshend had worked out a rough script. Occasionally, Church was asked to improvise at the piano to cover the play's dramatic action, and each time the directorial preparations took a leap forward, the music would adapt and be plugged into what became the score. The score is now roughly the size of a wedding cake.

For the original staging at the La Jolla Playhouse, an eight-piece ensemble relied on electronic synthesizers to produce exotic percussion sounds and string orchestrations. Moving to Broadway meant working with New York unions and expanding the ensemble to meet a minimum of twenty-five working players. Luckily, the idea for using a second French horn had materialized months before, when a substitute sat in on a La Jolla rehearsal and produced pleasingly fat melodies. The remote-control string quartet and two percussionists—one for tympani and gong, one for tambourine and triangle—replaced the synthesizers that had initially replaced them. Three keyboardists were contracted, one whose instrument was programmed to act as an acoustic piano, the others playing true synthesizers. (Samplers, which store sounds digitally and are triggered by keyboards, give the troupe flexibility to replicate effects like the odd reverse-clave sound heard in "Amazing Journey.") All this left wide berth for drums, played by veteran Luther Rix with reverent attention to the original performances by Keith Moon. The musicians admitted into the pit needed a distinctive and powerful sound, but also the formal schooling that enabled them to stop on a dime and respond to a conductor's directives. Hence the irony: well-trained "legitimate" players with an empathic understanding

Musical Director Joe Church in rehearsal, New York, 1993.

of that philistine cultural warhorse called rock-and-roll.

The grand features of *Tommy*'s music are technically the simplest but require the most conviction from the performers to do the piece justice—this is, in effect, how legitimate rock-and-roll works. An overture typically contains motifs of pieces which are to follow; the new "Overture" is extended to include flashes of the acoustic-guitar chords from the verse of "Pinball Wizard" which, second only to a smashed instrument, are a Pete Townshend signature. These "suspended" chords are common major shapes with the fourth degree of their corresponding scale added. When that suspension is removed and the chord again becomes major, the resolution is among the most powerful cadences in all of music. On hearing it once, the ear takes the bait. Twice, it becomes a theme. From that moment, the mere hint of such a tonality has completely—and perhaps subconsciously—enmeshed music and listener.

In "Christmas" a piano plays the suspended chords, with choral reinforcement popping up between the verses. Unlike its performance on the original album, where substantive gaps are left in the story line, the song is tied into elaborate church imagery. Young Tommy's angst is pronounced in this stage version through a recurring "See Me, Feel Me" soliloquy by a spectral older Tommy, but even more so by his parents' longing to resuscitate his senses. At one point amid the confusion, Mr. and Mrs. Walker face each other and sing notes which suggest the suspensions, bare and unaccompanied, and the wedge of their helplessness is driven home hard.

There may be a timely statement about domestic atrocity in repositioning the lubricious antics of Uncle Ernie after "Christmas," but as a musical move, the angular "Fiddle About" provides a respite to what has come before. "Fiddle About" and "Cousin Kevin," written by Entwistle, are reversed in order and made less discrete than on the Who's original recording; the latter number is introduced with the ominous *Jaws*-style knell of arpeggiated chords (suspended, incidentally) and sung at Tommy by the odious troupe that will lead him to pinball and suddenly worship him beside the machine as he plays. The impaired boy becomes a "Sensation" long before he can even experience one himself, with the older Tommy adding the epithet "I am the light" to his one other line of pre-cure dialogue, "Happy Birthday," before he disappears into darkness behind the stanchion. (In a not-too-mystic coincidence, *I Am* and *Happy Birthday* are also titles of two early seventies Townshend records dedicated to *Tommy* avatar Meher Baba.)

Jonathan Dokuchitz (Captain Walker) treating his throat during rehearsal, New York, 1993.

Roger Daltrey on tour, 1989.

With its stuttering unisons between guitar and bass, "Acid Queen" typified the composing and playing that would develop wildly in the birth of Townshend's second opera, 1974's *Quadrophenia*. A battery of modern-style guitar histrionics leads into this account of Mr. Walker's efforts to cure his son with the help of a crazed prostitute dealing psychedelic drugs. Broadway has done away with the original recording's ten-minute "Underture" and extracted the "Sparks" theme—its bassline more mincing than John Entwistle would ever have played it—to accompany young Tommy's failing a music therapy test in a call-and-response exchange with the band. Once "Pinball Wizard" is introduced by tense guitar chords, the stage widens for a climactic treatment of that most famous piece, with flashing machines and the chorus' servile choreography, until audience and ensemble alike are beckoned to intermission with resonances of fierce, Townshendian strumming.

The second act of *Tommy* is less about music than spectacle, dialogue and resolution, where vocal performances become crucial to the effective presentation of the story. Some syntactical adjustments make sense: A specialist fears Tommy's shock "*if*," rather than *when* "he suddenly can hear and speak and see." Not prize-winning grammar, but it removes the distraction that this doctor, in addition to being expensive, also practices clairvoyance.

"Tommy Can You Hear Me?" is sung not by the loving Mrs. Walker but by a mocking chorus of street toughs, ostensibly to better set off "I Believe My Own Eyes," in which Tommy's parents assess the strain his illness has placed on their relationship. Composed for this production by Townshend, it borrows generously from the harmonies of the play's flagship pieces and clearly articulates the sort of sentimentality that Broadway needed from the revised *Tommy*. It's nice, and familiar, but lest we've blocked out the first ninety minutes of hospital scenes, tears and Tommy-can-you-hear-me's, "I Believe" recounts tacitly that this show focuses on the earnestness of these characters to relieve their son of a sickness induced more by circumstance than neglect; when Tommy is finally cured, his alienation from his mother and father is that much more confusing. The song is delivered in the great theatrical tradition of the vocalist's rich, quavering vibrato, which is an operatic formality seldom allowed rock singers; were *Tommy*'s stage performers as untrained or as detached from the proprieties of high culture as the Who were when they wrote

121

it, the result on stage would be nearly unredeemable.

The moment his mirror is smashed and Tommy exclaims "I'm free" is precisely when listeners familiar with previous interpretations fall into the wide rift between the Who and the reformulated *Tommy*. Once cast through skies and scapes of enlightenment, the boy now sees freedom embodied in his family's sitting room, and wordless melodies replace the chorus of "How can we follow?" heard from his disciples on the original recording. In Townshend's new vision, Tommy is just a star. The one-time "messiah" now revels in mortality, and the reaction of his followers is so deliberate and delayed that the '69 record's treatment of religious fervor seems updated as a jab at the unavoidable nineties media-hype machine. Slowly played strains of "Fiddle About" announce Uncle Ernie's self-appointment as huckster, and Tommy rises to the pinball pulpit, then the talk-show circuit. He rejects exaltation with a spoken statement heard frequently in the Who canon—both Townshend and Entwistle wrote songs entitled "(I've) Had Enough"—and as if to parody his tarnished self-actualization, the powerful "I'm Free" chords are dragged out in languorous sympathy.

The masses want the opiate; they reject Tommy's reality for the illusion of being led along the same shining path. This perspective on his journey simplifies the spiritual matters being addressed, but turns out a fair comment on the media-obsessed nineties. However, when Tommy is finally reunited with his most venial oppressors—his extended family—and the guitar chords of "Pinball Wizard" are reprised to a predictably explosive ovation, the audience sees itself in a huge upstage mirror. All very neat and charming indeed: in the words of Sally Simpson's ever-nurturing mother, just "be what you'll be."

It's difficult not to feel proprietary about the initial experience of any work, especially one with such a pronounced spiritual core. Tommy's mandate for the nineties isn't to transcend but to cope, with the implication that his journey was nothing more than an unfortunate diversion. The classic tale really does play second fiddle in this musical. Because *Tommy* came fully loaded with a plot and songs proven through repeated playings at live performances, in films and on radio, the record's most striking iconographic features could be easily laid bare, scrutinized and reconceived to suit the taste of a wider, less familiar audience—even the composer understands that the story's current success is an attribute of that transformation. But where *Tommy* was once

"Since the demise of sophisticated big band jazz as our pop music we have swung to drums. We drive to drums, make love to drums and cook and eat to drums. The electric guitar has been both the strings and bass of rock, but drums are simply everywhere. Everywhere except in great music theatre. I hope to change that. And so does everyone who is working on this show."

—**Pete Townshend**

Tommy drummer Luther Rix in rehearsal, New York, 1993.

McAnuff and Church confer with former Beatles album producer George Martin (center), at the *Tommy* cast album recording session, The Hit Factory, New York, 1993.

prismatic, with a symbol visible from every angle—selfish autocracy, religious opportunism, the "blinding" notion of rejecting common senses to find higher answers—it now exists within very specific visual and conceptual boundaries. Broadway's hero is confused by power, though the answers he seeks are implicit in his disease, and in our reactions to these characters' many failings and fallacious choices. Townshend's pop philosophy was successful because it said so much without leading us by the nose through one specific interpretation—of all of those available, to settle on the ravages of toxic parenting just doesn't cut it. Tommy's real message? Perhaps that, ultimately, liberation comes with an understanding that we can only possess true vision without paying mind to life's spectacle.

Tommy might well have heeded Mrs. Simpson. Like great show tunes and opera, he was born to make sense in song. So the question isn't, "Can rock go to the theatre?" but rather "Does rock need the theatre?" Rock opera is intentionally vague; its symbols don't need explication.

"You hope what happens in the theatre is that by viewing it people make the jump to exercise their minds and think about the inner potential of the piece," says Pete Townshend. "We're talking about bringing *something* of rock-and-roll to Broadway. You can't bring it all because it won't work. Rock-and-roll won't work with the loop closed." Thankfully, Tommy's music retains its strength even this far along. It's still a revealing sketch of every theatregoer's daily helping of ridicule, glorification and remuneration for being different.

Matt Resnicoff is senior editor of Musician *magazine.*

Scene 17: The Streets of London, 1961–1963

(Against a lurid backdrop of Fleet Street at night, a reporter joins Uncle Ernie, who produces a photograph.)

UNCLE ERNIE *(spoken)*
What you've stumbled upon here, my son, could be ginormous—a story on a par with the opening of King Tut's tomb or the *Hindenburg* disaster. Happily, I was able to capture the moment of young Tommy Walker's miraculous recovery for all posterity—right there in black and white. One would think that such a valuable snap would be worth a hundred quid… but it's yours for a mere fifty.

(The photo is a bad one of Tommy holding up his hand to the camera. The reporter gives Uncle Ernie back the photograph.)

UNCLE ERNIE
I could, of course, just hand the Nobel prize over to one of your Fleet Street colleagues from, say, the *Mirror* or the *Times* or the *Guardian*.

(The reporter walks away.)

UNCLE ERNIE
What about for the price of a bottle of Scotch?

(The reporter exits.)

(Tommy enters, takes the picture out of Ernie's hand, looks at it and tosses it into the air. Suddenly, his picture is everywhere. In front of a background of black-and-white printing presses, a rather bored, middle-aged news vendor enters, hawking the tabloids headlining Tommy's recovery.)

VENDOR
Deaf, dumb and blind kid in miracle cure. Read about it here. Deaf, dumb and blind kid. Special section. Final edition. Deaf, dumb and blind kid in miracle cure.

MIRACLE CURE

(As the picture is repeatedly projected in the background, the local lads enter, delighted with the news. The lads surround the News Vendor and swipe his papers, one by one.)

LOCAL LADS   Extra! Extra!
Read all about it!
The pinball wizard in a miracle cure!
Extra! Extra!
Read all about it!
Extra!

(Uncle Ernie buys a paper and furiously leafs through it. The lads go off as the newly conscious Tommy rides in on a pinball machine.)

London Newspapers   1969

THE LATE FIFTIES AND EARLY SIXTIES WERE A PERIOD OF tremendous growth and change for the English media. Wartime restrictions on newsprint were finally lifted in 1956, and competition intensified both within the print-media world and from the twentieth century's newest wonder: television.

English national newspapers during this period had three subdivisions: "quality," "middle market" and "mass-market tabloids." Quality papers, such as the *Daily Telegraph* and the *Times*, held their readers, but the bottom began to fall out for the middle-market newspapers. Mass-market tabloids showed the most growth; the greatest circulation increase from 1955 to 1965 was won by the *Daily Mirror*.

Mirror was an apt title for a newspaper at this time; the tradition of national and international political reporting of the World War II era had given way to reflecting what was more on the public's mind—features or special-interest stories such as Tommy's "miracle cure." From the sensational to the trivial, the postwar society placed news emphasis on human interest.

And sensation was hard to avoid. The nationalized, austere British Broadcasting Corporation (BBC) gained a new competitor in 1955: Independent Television (ITV). Funded exclusively by advertising, ITV's gambits for winning the popular audience brought new vigor to the expanding television industry. In the early 1960s, in every British home, a new consciousness was being forged in the bluish glow of black-and-white TV; Britain had entered the age of "mass media."

—Chad Sylvain, Tommy *Dramaturge*

"It's customary to invite the press in during
rehearsals for a moment of show and tell.
Of course, you never can predict how the press
will react, and often you have to beg them to
come. But for Tommy, interest was so great we
were forced to be selective about our invita-
tions. This was the first time MTV and VH1 ever
covered a Broadway press call."

        —Adrian Bryan-Brown, Press Representative

SENSATION (REPRISE)

TOMMY   You'll feel me coming,
        A new vibration.
        From afar you'll see me.
        I'm a sensation…
        I'm a sensation!

        Soon you'll see me. Can't you feel me?
        I'm coming…

REPORTERS *(rushing in to surround Tommy)*
        Sensation… Sensation.

TOMMY   Send your troubles dancing;
        you know the answer.

TOMMY   I'm coming…   REPORTERS   Sensation…
        I'm coming…   Sensation!

REPORTERS Sensation… Sensation!

(The year 1961 is projected on the stage. The Walkers enter and are surrounded by reporters.)

MRS. WALKER *(spoken)*
It's true, our son doesn't come round anymore. We never get to see him. I do worry sometimes, you know, that we're the only ones who really understand and all… but we're grateful, of course—grateful for his transformation.

MR. WALKER
Which is a better word for it. We don't like the use of the word "miracle" one bit. He simply got well. That's the extent of it. And his mother and I never gave up the faith through all the years. Not once.

MRS. WALKER
We just hope he's happy. It seems he's become all the rage today, doesn't it?

(Reporters rush to surround Tommy's machine. The local lads appear in security-guard uniforms. A uniformed Cousin Kevin seems to be in charge.)

REPORTERS Sensation… Sensation!
        Sensation… Sensation!

(The year 1962 is projected on the stage. Tommy pivots, pulls back the plunger and fires.)

COUSIN KEVIN *(being interviewed; his image appears on video monitors above the stage)*
Those of us who've known my cousin a long time, his friends from before like, we're providing the necessary protection. So as far as family relations are concerned, all I'm saying is he's been very good to me. Very good. And I for one am glad I can be of some assistance. I believed in him from the beginning, right from the very start. I know what it was like. I was there.

ALL   Sensation… Sensation!
                        Sensation… Sensation!

(The year 1963 is projected on the stage.)

ALL   Sensation… Sensation!
                        Sensation… Sensation!
                        Ahhh, Sensation…
                        Sensation!

(A television studio appears and Tommy sits with the talk-show hostess. Their images appear on video screens.)

TOMMY *(to the interviewer)*
I won't answer that. I want to be very clear with you. I won't answer any questions about my personal life. So leave off.

(The Walkers fade quietly into the background and go off.)

As for people's interest… I got a lot out of playing… learned a lot from it, you know. It's all I had, really. And my dreams. It's like… people want me to pass that on in some way. So that's what I'm trying to do. Pass it on.

"Not wanting to choreograph this scene around wires on the stage, we buried modern video cameras inside these early 60s' cameras, and achieved the impression of a live feed without the umbilical cord of wires. It's the first time microwave video cameras have been used this way on Broadway."

—Des McAnuff, Director

Roger Daltrey   1975

I'M FREE/PINBALL WIZARD (REPRISE)

TOMMY   I could tell you what it takes
               To feel the highest high.
               You'd laugh and say "Nothing's that simple!"

(Tommy sings directly into the camera and a close-up of his face appears on the video screen.)

               I'm free… I'm free…
               And I'm waiting for you to follow me!

(The studio disappears and only Tommy and his security guards remain on stage. Tommy is inventing a public self, Tommy the star, as images of the younger Tommys, his parents, the murder, pinball, the brain scan and finally his new self flash before us.)

TOMMY   He stands like a statue,
               Becomes part of the machine.
               Feeling all the bumpers,
               Always playing clean.
               He plays by intuition;
               The digit counters fall.
               That deaf, dumb and blind kid
               Sure plays a mean pinball!

               He ain't got no distractions,
               Can't hear those buzzers and bells,
               Can't see those lights a-flashin',
               Plays by sense of smell.
               Always gets a replay,
               'N' never tilts at all…
               That deaf, dumb and blind kid
               Sure plays a mean pinball!

TOMMY & SECURITY GUARDS
               He's a pinball wizard.
               There has to be a twist.
               A pinball wizard,
               S'got such a supple wrist.

FOR MANY YEARS ROGER DALTREY WAS THE VOICE OF Tommy on stage and then the embodiment of the deaf, dumb and blind boy in Ken Russell's 1975 film. Now there's another Tommy and Pete Townshend has visceral reactions to both. "If I created the character of Tommy as a seeker, Roger Daltrey realized him as a finder. Working behind Roger playing Tommy is to feel piloted by a Stealth bomber finding its target; no one quite knows where it is coming from, you can't see it on the radar, but when it appears and hits home it blows you away. Michael Cerveris has created a new Tommy. Less a driven, vengeful zealot—more a self-willed victim of an absurd crime of passion who becomes wise through experience. Both Roger and Michael have produced stunning variations on my original idea. "

DIRECTOR DES MCANUFF AND SET DESIGNER JOHN ARNONE wanted to underscore the climactic moment when pinwheel wizard Tommy plays his game in Act II. His bucking bronco of a machine was supposed to heat up, send out sparks and finally catch on fire and explode. Enter the special-effects designers, Jauchem & Meeh, Inc. "We decided to make the machine flame several times and then short-circuit and explode. Now the rhythm goes something like, flame, flame, flame, bang," says Greg Meeh. "But no matter how loud we got the bang in the shop, we always had to double the volume for the theatre." Loaded with about a hundred dollars' worth of explosives an hour before curtain and operated by an electrician who holds a qualifying certificate from the Fire Department, the exploding pinball machine is approved for safety by the Explosives Unit of the New York Fire Department and the Local Fire Battalion. "The riskiest thing about exploding the machine," says Meeh, "is doing it live, eight times a week in time with the music!"

COUSIN KEVIN & GUARDS

How do you think he does it?

TOMMY   I don't know.

COUSIN KEVIN & GUARDS

What makes him so good?

(A dazzling, mirrored pinball machine rises from the floor. Tommy, in a helmet that makes him deaf and blind again, mounts the machine and rides it as it twists and turns maniacally.)

COUSIN KEVIN & GUARDS

Even at my favorite table
He can beat my best.
His disciples lead him in
And he just does the rest.
He's got crazy flipper fingers;
Never seen him fall…
That deaf, dumb and blind kid
Sure plays a mean pinball!

(The pinball machine faces out with Tommy behind it. Suddenly, pulsing lights, shrieking buzzers and bells surround us, as if we were inside the guts of the machine. Tommy continues to play furiously as the pinball machine gyrates in an accelerating pyrotechnic fit. When the pinball machine finally explodes in a glorious, climactic fireball, Tommy steps back, victorious. Silence. And then the sound of a cheering crowd. In the glare of stadium lights, Tommy is now performing with his back to the audience on a raised platform in a stadium before an adoring crowd.)

TOMMY   I'm free… I'm free…
                And I'm waiting for you to follow me!

CROWD   How can we follow?
                How can we follow?

(Multiple video screens display the live action of Tommy's act before the crowd, as Cousin Kevin and the lads-turned-guards patrol the stage.)

SCENE 18: THE STADIUM: TOMMY'S HOLIDAY CAMP

———•———

(Uncle Ernie the merchandiser stands with a megaphone on a bridge made of videos and shamelessly works the crowd.)

UNCLE ERNIE *(spoken)*
Hello there, darlings!

TOMMY'S HOLIDAY CAMP

UNCLE ERNIE   I'm Tommy's Uncle Ernie,
               And I welcome you to Tommy's Holiday Camp!
               The camp with a difference!
               Never mind the weather!
               When you come to Tommy's, the holiday's forever!

               Get your Tommy T-shirts and your stickers
               And your Tommy mirrors to smash!
               Don't rush… keep steady!
               Have your money ready!
               Buy your way to heaven.
               That comes to one pound seven.
               Bless you, love.

               Buy your shades and ear plugs here!
               Keep in line. I've got a huge… supply.
               Get your Tommy record,
               You can really hear him talk!
               Tommy pics and badges…
               Half a nicker for the cork.

UNCLE ERNIE *(spoken)*
Watch this, then.
(He does a little dance while showing videos of Tommy merchandise.)

"Holiday Camp is just a merchandising scheme, a name for the tour. There's no camp—it's just Ernie outside of the concert hawking stuff to make money, to capitalize on Tommy. We were thinking of this scene as an encapsulation of the rapacity that surrounds rock stars or any famous person."

—Paul Kandel, *Uncle Ernie*

The Last Word

No day of rehearsal was complete until director Des McAnuff gave the actors the notes which he had dictated to his assistant during each scene. Usually exhausted, the cast would pay close attention to the trenchant comments that ranged from suggestions about particular performances to acting theory in general:

"Without letting it get sentimental, I want you to feel sadness."

"The hardest thing on stage is to maintain a sense of wonder, astonishment, incredulity. That's what I want you to do."

"Truth is not a sometimes thing—anytime we're in a scene, I want honest work."

"Unless a gesture really reinforces the line, you're better off staying with the line. Otherwise the movement can really dissipate the energy."

"Remember all the basic Tommy principles—be careful about indicating (which is suicide) and be careful about not emoting—it's more English to be more reserved. Besides, it's that contained emotion that's so devastating."

"You girls were so great in 'Pinball.' It was like something out of 'Women behind Bars.'"

"I want to feel like you need her— that physical attraction that goes beyond attraction—it validates your very soul."

"We discovered this in high school: The most important thing is your hair."

"Watch the hand gesture—that's where you look like Benito Mussolini."

"The adjustment you made in that scene is what gives me faith in storytelling. I was actually quite affected myself. It's starting to feel really rich."

UNCLE ERNIE The camp with a difference!
       Never mind the weather!
       When you come to Tommy's, the holiday's forever!

UNCLE ERNIE *(spoken)*
This is your chance! Tommy's Holiday Camp is coming to your town. At eight tonight—Tommy, live on stage! You lucky people!

(Tommy's face appears on the video screens as the guards threateningly escort a somewhat sheepish Uncle Ernie from the stage as Cousin Kevin watches approvingly. He stays as we are introduced to the Simpson household.)

SCENE 19: SALLY'S HOUSE/THE STADIUM

———●———

(The security guards are gathered at the edge of the stage, confronting the audience. Tommy is on the podium behind them with his back to the guards and the audience.)

SALLY SIMPSON

COUSIN KEVIN Outside the house, Mr. Simpson announces
       Sally can't go to the meeting.
       He goes on cleaning his blue Rolls-Royce
       And she runs inside a-weeping.
       She gets to her room and cries on a picture,
       Always keeps it by her.
       She picks up a book of her father's life
       And throws it on the fire.

(The videos show stadium crowds and Tommy's face as a weeping Sally is joined at her dressing table by her mother.)

SALLY & MR. & MRS. SIMPSON
       She knew from the start,
       Deep down in her heart,
       That she and Tommy were worlds apart...

SALLY & MRS. SIMPSON
       But her mother said, "Never mind; your part
       Is to be
       What you'll be."

SALLY   Tommy's gonna beat his best tonight;
       I just have to see him play.
       I feel so bad; I'm sorry, Dad.
       Gonna sneak out anyway.

"In order to get up there and act like a rock star, you have to feel legitimate. What I'm drawing on is the experience of being on stage and playing with Pete Townshend. That was the ultimate rock-and-roll experience for me!"

—Michael Cerveris, Tommy

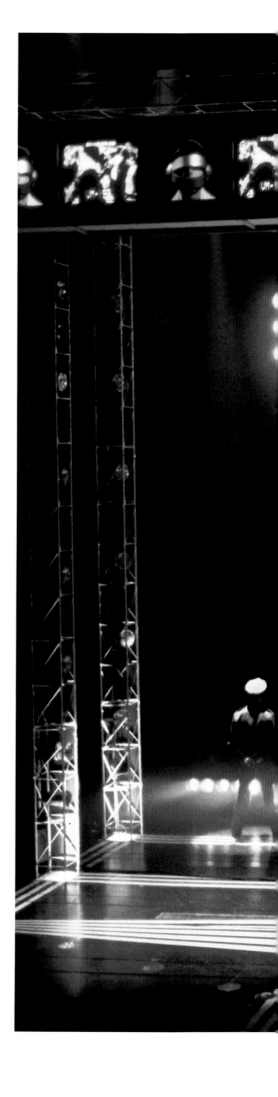

London   Circa 1965

FOR SALLY SIMPSON'S BROAD-
WAY DEBUT, PETE TOWNSHEND
made a deliberate effort to change
her character. "In the original
Tommy, Sally was not quite as
much a groupie as she is now. She
was just young, impressionable,
looking for roots, connection, a
place. Our new Sally is a modern
girl. She wants it all. She wants
the backstage experience, and the
front stage experience, too. And
she wants answers from Tommy.
I also believe that she wants
Tommy himself.

    "It is the fact that he doesn't
acknowledge that, or even seem to
care about it, that I believe justi-
fies the journalists' and observers'
anger and final dismissal of him.
It's not that they believe in backstage sex, just that Sally got badly
beaten up and they believe that
Tommy owes her an answer that
will provide salvation."

> I've spent all day doin' up my hair;
> I've gotta look exactly right.
> Maybe he'll see that I can be free
> And I'll get backstage tonight.

(Sally does herself up and rushes off past her parents.)

MR. & MRS. SIMPSON
> She knew from the start,
> Deep down in her heart,
> That she and Tommy were worlds apart…
> But her mother said, "Never mind; your part
> Is to be
> What you'll be."

(Sally, hair blowing in the wind, rides across the stage on her motor scooter.)

TWO GUARDS   She lands at six and the gig is a-rocking;
> The devil's out tonight.
> The band cuts loose and the stage is a-knocking
> But Sally just sits real tight.
> She grabs her chair—she's hot to dance
> Right down in the very front row.
> Then a slick DJ who is pissing his pants
> Runs on and says:

DJ   Here we go…

(Sally appears in the first row of the audience, eager to jump up on stage.)

GUARDS   The crowd goes crazy
> As Tommy hits the stage!
> Little Sally is lost
> As the police boss
> The crowd back in a rage! Wooooo!

(Tommy stands on a high podium doing his act while his face appears on the video screens. The guards surround him in an unbreakable line.)

SALLY SIMPSON

> A flash of fire—the whole place stops.
> Tommy is a tranquilizer,
> But Sally's so hot—she risks a shot
> And jumps up on the riser.

(Sally rushes past the guards and climbs up onto Tommy's podium, where she throws her scarf around his neck.)

COUSIN KEVIN She's up there now—she's hit the top.
> She brushes his handsome face.
> Tommy whirls around as a uniformed man
> Ushers her from the stage.

(Tommy turns and unconsciously knocks Sally from the stage. The guards below grab her and beat her viciously.)

THE GUARDS She knew from the start,
> Deep down in her heart,
> That she and Tommy were worlds apart.
> But her mother said "Never mind; your part
> Is to be
> What you'll be."

(Tommy leaps off the podium, pushes through the security guards and kneels beside her, realizing how completely out of control everything's gotten. He rocks her in his lap.)

TOMMY Be.........
> What you'll be,
> What you'll be,
> What you'll be,
> What you'll be,
> What you'll be.

"I made several changes in Sally's lyrics, but the main thing was to actually mention the word "backstage," in the line "I hope I can get backstage tonight." Her target is to be with Tommy, even though she's not particularly enamored with him; she's really enamored with fame and success."

—Pete Townshend

"The louts didn't exist at all until we thought
them up for the musical, and I think they've
become really critical to the story. They actually
grow up with Tommy, and he, in a sense,
becomes one of them. Ironically, although they
abuse him, it's through this interaction that
a kind of love for him comes about. Finally, as
his security guards, they protect him. The
louts turned into six wonderful through-line
characters, and I'm very fond of them."

—Des McAnuff, Director

SCENE 20: 22 HEATHFIELD GARDENS

———————•———————

(Tommy looks at the guards, and the crowd, which has gone silent.)

TOMMY *(to the crowd)*
I've had enough. I think I'm gonna go back home now. Suss everything out. I'm going home. But… you can all come if you like. Yeah. You've all got your families, right? Come and be a part of mine for a bit. See what it's been like for me.

(The guards look dumbfounded at Tommy's invitation to the crowd as the pieces of 22 Heathfield Gardens assemble behind them.)

WELCOME

(Still cradling the wounded Sally, Tommy sings to the audience.)

TOMMY *(quietly cynical)*
>Come to my house.
>Be one of my family's people.
>Lovely bright home…
>We're dancing all night,
>Never sleeping.

(Tommy helps Sally to her feet and disarms the security guards.)

>Milkman, come in!
>And you, baker!
>Little old lady, welcome!
>And you, shoemaker!
>
>Come to this house!
>Into this house!

(He begins herding the guards, the crowd and Sally to his parent's house.)

TOMMY & GUARDS
>Come to this house;
>Be one of us.
>Make this your house;
>Be one of us.

(Standing in front of his door with Sally in his arms, Tommy instructs the guards.)

TOMMY
>You can help
>To collect some more in.
>Young and old people,
>Let's get them all in!

(Videos and projections appear, first of small groups, then lines, then crowds of people.)

TOMMY
>Come to this house!
>Into this house!

(Not having seen him at home since his cure, the Walkers and Uncle Ernie are startled to see Tommy bringing home a crowd of guards, reporters and the battered Sally Simpson. Tommy leaves Sally with them and rushes out to bring more people in as the reporters mill around the house.)

TOMMY *(to the guards)*

> Ask along that man who's wearing a carnation.
> Bring every single person
> From Victoria Station.
> Go into that hospital
> And bring nurses and patients.
> Everyone go home and fetch your relations!

TOMMY & CROWD

> Come to this house;
> Be one of this family's people.
> Lovely bright home…
> Dancing all night, never sleeping.

COUSIN KEVIN *(spoken)*
Sir, there's more at the door.

COUSIN KEVIN & GUARDS

> There's more at the door.
> There's more at the door.
> There's more at the door.

(A cutout backdrop of the crowd flies in, leading us to believe that the stadium audience and crowds of people off the street fill the Walkers' house. The monitors show crowds surging down a London street.)

ALL

> There's more at the door.
> There's more at the door.
> There's more at the door.
> There's more at the door.
> There's more…

TOMMY

> We need more room.
> Build an extension!
> We'll all work together.
> Spare no expense now.

(Mrs. Walker brings Sally in from the bedroom. Tommy crosses to her.)

TOMMY *(to Sally)*

> Come to this house;
> Be one of us.
> Come into this house;
> Be one of us.
>
> Come to our house.
> Come to me now!

(Tommy sits Sally down next to him on the sofa, as the reporters crowd around to capture Tommy's answer to Sally's question. Their image is picked up by the television camera and displayed on screens all over the stage.)

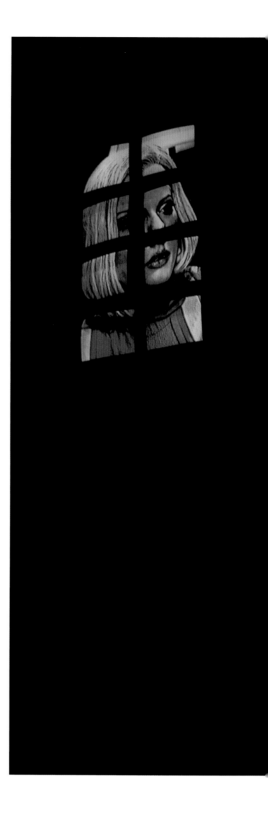

"*What's fascinating about the video in* Tommy *is how the live element is combined with camera and laser-disc images. The trick is in balancing the video images with what's happening on stage so that one doesn't overshadow the other. Ultimately, when done well, the combination leads to incredible moments of enhanced reality.*"

—**Batwin + Robin,** *Video Designers*

"*Essentially, the way to communicate with the public is through the press—you can invite the entire country into your house through the cameras. Rock stars know this and we were trying to use rock-and-roll mythology and history to inform our staging here. The background is reminiscent of the* Sgt. Pepper *album art, and we used video images of crowds pouring down a typical London street, borrowed in part from* A Hard Day's Night *where fans pursue the Beatles.*"

—Des McAnuff, Director

SALLY'S QUESTION

SALLY How can we share the great sights you are seeing?
Hear all the glorious music you hear?

(Sally waits for Tommy to answer; he just shakes his head.)

How can we be a small part of your being?
Why do you seem so alive when you're near?

(Tommy doesn't answer.)

SALLY *(spoken)*
Tell us. Tell us now. How can we be more like you?

TOMMY
Why would you want to be more like me?
For fifteen years I was waiting for what you've already got.

SALLY
What's that?

TOMMY
All this. In my dreams I was seeing it, hearing it, feeling it. Those are the true miracles and you have them already.

SALLY
I don't understand.

TOMMY
The point is not for you to be more like me. The point is… I'm finally more like you. I can't be who you want me to be.

(The crowd of reporters, guards and the family are all asking a confusion of questions. Tommy looks around him and stands up impatiently, to address the camera and the crowd.)

WE'RE NOT GOING TO TAKE IT

TOMMY Welcome to this house;
I think I *now* know why you're here.
You wanna be like Tommy?
I'm glad you're not, I hope that's clear.
You shouldn't try to ape my show,
It isn't just pinball.
You don't need to claim
A share of my pain…
You're normal, after all.

(He crosses over to the guards.)

TOMMY You might as well get drunk.
So sorry—I've got you sussed.
No instant high for free here.
This is a bust!
I didn't live out some fairy story,
Some rags-to-riches crawl…

I couldn't see,
I couldn't hear,
I couldn't talk at all.

(Tommy turns back to the mirror, as his face appears on the videos. Disgusted by his answer, the guards and reporters start to turn against Tommy.)

SECURITY GUARDS & REPORTERS

We're not gonna take it.
We're not gonna take it.
We're not gonna take it.
We're not gonna take it.

We're not gonna take it,
Never did and never will.
We're not gonna take it.
Gonna break it, gonna shake it,
Let's forget it, better still.

(The family seems confused and mystified, the guards becoming openly hostile.)

TOMMY *(to the crowd)*

You don't need to hear me;
You've got ideas of your own.
Don't have to come and cheer me;
That's something you've outgrown.
You don't need to see me;
Your vision makes the scene.
Don't let Uncle Ernie make you play
On Tommy's old machine!

CROWD

We're not gonna take it.
We're not gonna take it.
We're not gonna take it.
We're not gonna take it.

(The crowd begins to disperse; the reporters start to pack up and leave, as do the security guards whom Cousin Kevin tries to reassure in vain.)

CROWD

We're not gonna take it,
Never did and never will.
Won't take your derision
And, as far as we can tell,
We don't have to take you…
Never did and never will.
We're not gonna take you.
We forsake you, maybe rape you;
Let's forget you, better still…

"Tommy talks about his appreciation for the miracle of existence because he experiences life the way few of us do—after all, he's been born whole at twenty. But with the rejection of the crowd, he experiences for the first time the dark side, which threatens his recovery for a moment."

—Des McAnuff, Director

*"After the crowd rejects him, Tommy is pulled
back toward his previous state and attempts
to go back into the mirror. At that point
his smaller self becomes his spiritual guide
just as the Narrator had been for little Tommy
in the beginning of the play. He raises his
hand and smiles at me as if to say 'Stay there.
It's okay, you're strong enough to embrace
and accept the world.'"*

—Michael Cerveris, Tommy

THE GUARDS   We forsake you…
                     Let's forget you, better still…

(The crowd gradually abandons Tommy until Sally is the only fan left. Tommy turns to her, but she walks out after the others. As Tommy crosses back to the mirror, the family fears he may have a relapse.)

(The image in the mirror is now the ten-year-old Tommy. The two Tommys reach for each other tenderly. Everything else fades away.)

SEE ME, FEEL ME/LISTENING TO YOU (REPRISE)

TOMMY & TEN-YEAR-OLD TOMMY
                See me, feel me,
                Touch me, heal me.
                See me, feel me,
                Touch me, heal me.

                See me, feel me,
                Touch me, heal me.
                See me, feel me,
                Touch me, heal me.

(The image of the boy fades away and Tommy is left gazing at his adult self. He turns towards his family, who are a bit wary of him.)

TOMMY   Listening to you, I get the music;
                 Gazing at you, I get the heat.
                 Following you, I climb the mountain;
                 I get excitement at your feet.

>Right behind you, I see the millions;
>On you, I see the glory.
>From you, I get opinions;
>From you, I get the story.

(One by one, Tommy embraces Cousin Kevin, Uncle Ernie, and his parents—with acceptance and understanding. They respond hesitantly but are finally exhilarated by this reunion. The family joins the song, even Cousin Kevin.)

TOMMY & FAMILY

>Listening to you, I get the music;
>Gazing at you, I get the heat.
>Following you, I climb the mountain;
>I get excitement at your feet.

>Right behind you, I see the millions.
>On you, I see the glory.
>From you, I get opinions;
>From you, I get the story.

(22 Heathfield Gardens disassembles and the family is joined by others they've met along the way. They face the audience.)

ALL

>Listening to you, I get the music;
>Gazing at you, I get the heat.
>Following you, I climb the mountain;
>I get excitement at your feet.

>Right behind you, I see the millions;
>On you, I see the glory.
>From you, I get opinions;
>From you, I get the story.

(The others leave the stage as Tommy remains alone with his four-year-old and ten-year-old selves flanking him as he looks out through an invisible mirror.)

THE END

"Tommy's music is inherently theatrical. It is the momentum behind the story, providing constantly rising climaxes that drive the play to a sense of resolution. And as in great drama, the end is at once a conclusion and a new beginning."

—Joe Church, Musical Director

Capturing Rock-and-Roll and the Passions of 1969

Frank Rich

The following review appeared in the New York Times *on April 23, 1993, the morning after* Tommy's *opening night:*

The Broadway musical has never been the same since rock-and-roll stole its audience and threw it into an identity crisis. For three decades, from the moment *Meet the Beatles* usurped the supremacy of such Broadway pop as *Hello, Dolly!*, the commercial theater has desperately tried to win back the Young (without alienating their elders) by watering down rock music, simulating rock music and ripping off rock music. A result has been a few scattered hits over the years, typified by *Hair* and *Jesus Christ, Superstar*, most of which have tamed the rock-and-roll revolution rather than spread it throughout Times Square.

Until now.

Tommy, the stunning new stage adaptation of the 1969 rock opera by the British group the Who, is at long last the authentic rock musical that has eluded Broadway for two generations. A collaboration of its original principal author, Pete Townshend, and the director, Des McAnuff, this show is not merely an entertainment juggernaut, riding at full tilt on the visual and musical highs of its legendary pinball iconography and irresistible tunes, but also a surprisingly moving resuscitation of the disturbing passions that made *Tommy* an emblem of its era. In the apocalyptic year of 1969, *Tommy* was the unwitting background music for the revelation of the My Lai massacre, the Chicago Seven trial, the Charles Manson murders. Those cataclysmic associations still reverberate within the piece, there to be tapped for the Who's generation, even as the show at the St. James is so theatrically fresh and emotionally raw that newcomers to *Tommy* will think it was born yesterday.

In a way, it was. Though the voices and pit band of this *Tommy* faithfully reproduce the 1969 double album, adding merely one song ("I Believe My Own Eyes"), a few snippets of dialogue and some extended passages of underscoring, the production bears no resemblance to the Who's own concert performances of the opera (which culminated in an appearance at the Metropolitan Opera House in 1970) or to Ken Russell's pious, gag-infested 1975 film adaptation. Instead of merely performing the songs or exploiting them as cues for general riffs of dance and psychedelia, the evening's creators, who also include the choreographer Wayne Cilento and some extraordinary multimedia artists led by the brilliant set designer John Arnone, use their singing actors to flesh out the drama of *Tommy*. Better still, they excavate the fable's meaning until finally the opera's revised conclusion spreads catharsis like wildfire through the cheering house.

Both the story and its point are as simple as *Peter Pan* (with which

Tommy shares its London setting and some flying stunts by Foy). The show's eponymous hero is a boy who is stricken deaf, dumb and blind at the age of four after watching his father return from a World War II prisoners' camp to shoot his mother's lover. Tommy's only form of communication proves to be his latent wizardry at pinballs, a talent that soon turns him into a media sensation. As played by Michael Cerveris with the sleek white outfit, dark shades and narcissistic attitude of a rock star, the grown-up Tommy is nearly every modern child's revenge fantasy come true: the untouchable icon who gets the uncritical adulation from roaring crowds that his despised parents never gave him at home.

In this telling, Tommy is often played simultaneously by two child actors (representing him at ages four and ten) in addition to Mr. Cerveris. The isolated young Tommy's totemic, recurring cry of yearning—"See me, feel me, touch me, heal me"—flows repeatedly between inner child and grown man, giving piercing voice to the eternal childhood psychic aches of loneliness and lovelessness. It is this primal theme, expressed with devastating simplicity in Mr. Townshend's score and lyrics, that has made *Tommy* timeless, outlasting the Who itself (which disbanded in 1982). Yet it is the evil of the authority figures the hero must overcome—a distant father (Jonathan Dokuchitz), a dismissive mother (Marcia Mitzman), a sexually abusive Uncle Ernie (Paul Kandel) and various fascistic thugs—that also makes *Tommy* a poster-simple political statement reflecting the stark rage of the Vietnam era.

As staged by Mr. McAnuff, that anger is present but the story is kept firmly rooted in its own time, from the forties to the early sixties. The slide projections that drive the production design at first recreate in black-and-white the London of the blitz, then spill into the vibrant pop-art imagery of pinball

Reading the reviews, *Tommy* opening-night party, Marriott Marquis Hotel, New York, April 22, 1993.

Anita and Steve Shevett

Pete Townshend shares the Tony award for best musical score with Kander and Ebb, New York, June 6, 1993. *Tommy* won a total of five Tonys that night.

machines, early Carnaby Street and Andy Warhol painting before returning to black-and-white for televised crowd images that recall the early British rock explosion as witnessed on "The Ed Sullivan Show." Mr. Cilento's compact dances similarly advance from wartime jitterbugging to the fifties sock-hopping of early rock-and-roll movies to evocations of the Mod antics of *A Hard Day's Night* and its imitators in the sixties.

But the highly sophisticated theatrical style of this *Tommy*, which coalesces as a continuous wave of song, scenes, kaleidoscopic design and dance, owes everything to musical-theater innovations unknown until the mid-1970s. Mr. McAnuff, whose past Broadway works include the relatively stodgy *Big River* and *A Walk in the Woods*, shrewdly turns to examples set by such directors as Harold Prince, Michael Bennett and Robert Wilson. Here and there are echoes of the mock-documentary superstar sequences of *Evita* and *Dreamgirls*, in which abstract scaffolding and bridges suggest a show-biz firmament and a surging mob. As in those cinematic Prince and Bennett shows, the entire company becomes an undulating organism that defines the stage space and is always on the fly.

From Mr. Wilson, whose theater experiments have sometimes involved autistic boys eerily resembling the fictive Tommy, Mr. McAnuff and his designers take the notion of threading a few repeated images abstractly through the action: floating chairs, mirrors, the Union Jack, airplane propellers and disembodied Man Ray eyes, not to mention doors and windows reminiscent of sixties rock-album cover art and the hallucinogenic mythology such art canonized. (Sometimes the new incidental scoring takes some hints from Mr. Wilson's musical collaborator, Philip Glass.) These dreamy visual touchstones are constantly reshuffled and distorted throughout *Tommy* for subliminal effect, reaching their apotheosis in an inevitable (and superbly executed) set piece in which the entire theater becomes a gyrating pinball machine celebrating the rebel-

Tommy producers plan their marketing strategy, New York, May 1993.

Dodgers' Michael David and PACE's Scott Zeiger, opening-night party.

lious hero's "amazing journey" to newfound freedom.

Even in that blowout sequence, *Tommy* eschews the heavy visual spectacle of recent West End rock operas (and Broadway musicals) to keep its effects lithe and to the point. Often the most evocative sequences are spare and intimate: a candlelit Christmas dinner haunted by the ghosts of family horrors past, an abandoned urban lot in which the Acid Queen (Cheryl Freeman, paying persuasive vocal homage to Tina Turner) is more a feral junkie than a phantasmagoric Gypsy. Dominating the stage instead of being usurped by hardware, the performers can shine as well, from the dazzling Mr. Cerveris, who grows from melancholy youth to strutting pop belter, to Ms. Mitzman's powerfully sung mother, Mr. Kandel's sinister Uncle Ernie and the tireless ensemble, its youngest members included. When the time comes for the entire company to advance on the audience to sing the soaring final incantation— "Listening to you I get the music. Gazing at you I get the heat"—*Tommy* has done what rock-and-roll can do but almost never does in the theater: reawaken an audience's adolescent feelings of rebellion and allow them open-throated release. But reflecting the passage of time and Mr. Townshend's own mature age of forty-seven, this version takes a brave step further, concluding with a powerful tableau of reconciliation that lifts an audience of the 1990s out of its seats.

"Hope I die before I get old," sang the Who in "My Generation," its early hit single. A quarter-century or so later, Mr. Townshend hasn't got old so much as grown up, into a deeper view of humanity unthinkable in the late 1960s. Far from being another of Broadway's excursions into nostalgia, *Tommy* is the first musical in years to feel completely alive in its own moment. No wonder that for two hours it makes the world seem young.

Behind the Scenes

Rita D. Jacobs

In the early 1980s, Houston's PACE Theatrical Group and New York's Dodger Productions individually began to pursue the rights to produce Tommy *on stage. Ten years later, having prevailed in their quest for the rights, PACE and Dodger produced* Tommy *with the La Jolla Playhouse in La Jolla, California, in June 1992. On April 22, 1993, PACE Theatrical, Dodger Productions and New York's Kardana Productions brought* Tommy *to Broadway and the St. James Theatre where, almost to the day 50 years earlier,* Oklahoma! *had revolutionized the musical theatre.*

Musical theatre is a decidedly collaborative art. There may be shining stars, brilliant directors, genius playwrights, singular composers and even prescient producers, but none of them alone can make a show work.

Even before the actors are cast, the long process of harmonizing the talents of the people behind the scenes begins. For *Tommy* it all began before the book for the musical was complete, as discussions started between the designer, the director and the choreographer about how the show would look.

Director Des McAnuff and set designer John Arnone developed thematic ideas and metaphors as they worked.

"*Tommy* is about self-expression, about an adolescent finding a place for himself in a society that isn't necessarily friendly as he sees the door of adulthood looming in front of him," Arnone says. "And the set is about a structure, a house, because the core of the play is the family in a domestic

Stage Managers Frank Hartenstein (left) and Kelly Martindale (right) belong to the same union as the actors, although they never appear in front of the curtain. Essential members of the production crew, they ensure that the show goes smoothly—which covers everything from running the show and calling cues to directing traffic backstage to making sure that the actors get the appropriate number of breaks during rehearsal.

setting. We realized immediately the importance of themes such as child-parent relationships and the idea of separation—how one becomes an individual. The ideas are basic, but their echoes and vibrations are enormous.

"Two of the major features of the set are doors and windows, which keep you inside and safe. But beyond those doors and windows is something else, and this awakens a yearning to discover more—not only what's outside, but what's inside yourself; that is what is ultimately going to be the key that allows you to open the door to go to the outside."

In *Tommy*, the doors and windows either fly in or out or come on stage on tracks depending on the needs of the scene. But throughout the musical the stage is framed by steel structures which Arnone feels keep it defined but unobstructed.

"The trusswork is there because the motion of the piece is very fluid," he says. "Since the music doesn't stop, the actors are constantly in motion, and the stage has to be very open. You want to provide something on one hand which technically allows the action of the play to move very smoothly, but you also want to open up the idea of the piece to allow the audience's imagination to work. What I like to present are elements which are a sense-memory of actual visual elements, abstracted or selected in a very specific way. The audience understands the elements, and they're able to identify them and relate them to settings in their own mind that they may have encountered before. I try to stir a response based on personal experiences, and that's what I believe sets this design apart. Both Des and I believe in the intelligence of the audience—this experience is designed to happen for them."

Since the entire production is without music for only two minutes, the set also had to be created to work with Wayne Cilento's movement and dance choreography, all of which is integral to the dramatic situation. "We knew that we didn't want flamboyant choreography," says Cilento. "We wanted all the movement to be totally rooted in the drama. In any case, I'd rather dance for a reason. If it doesn't make sense for what's going on, I'd be the first to say 'Drop the choreography.'" Perhaps Cilento's restraint and

Pete Townshend's early concerns about whether or not the show "danced"—he was afraid that dance would tie *Tommy* to the existing traditions of Broadway musicals and it might fail to meet the comparison—are part of the reason why every movement in *Tommy* enhances the story.

As the basic plotting of set and movement occurs, other designers are working on providing an in-depth feeling of character, place and time. Costume designer David Woolard and scenic projection designer Wendall Harrington entered the creative dialogue early, and their discussions of color make a major difference in the way *Tommy* looks on stage today.

The actors in the overture, which is set against a backdrop of World War II, are costumed in black-and-white and shades of gray to evoke the effect of a wartime movie. When the scene switches to 22 Heathfield Gardens in London, the palette changes to normal colors to mark the point when the actual story begins. After Captain Walker shoots the lover and Tommy is traumatized, the colors become increasingly saturated and vivid to reflect Tommy's disturbed state of mind—the police appear in deep royal blue rather than navy and doctors and nurses are dressed in raspberry and chartreuse. Later, in the sixties, with the advent of Tommy's media acclaim, the color palette shifts to the black-and-white of newsprint and early television. This color scheme also recalls the earlier World War II palette and provides a color—or black and white—bookend for the production.

After the basic palette is determined, fine tuning the color is another process—truly collaborative, partly frustrating and always exciting. From the beginning Woolard envisioned the costumes in terms of color rather than style. "The color came first," he says, "and then it was secondary whether a character should be wearing a dress or a skirt and blouse. Although I work a lot in color, I had a stronger color reaction to *Tommy* than to any other show I've ever done."

Given this, it's not surprising that Harrington, who began work on the projections with color swatches provided by Woolard, had a color epiphany

"Throughout the process of designing the play we tried to travel a fine line between realism and something a bit more expressionistic—we were all really working towards creating a heightened sense of reality on stage."
—John Arnone, *Set Designer*

that shifted the look of *Tommy*. "I'd always felt that the audience needed some sympathy, some emotional bond to this boy, and you can do things like that with color," she says. "We had a color palette dominated by green, yellow and blue—harsh, bright colors—which were correct thematically, but emotionally there was something missing. And then I went to the Matisse show at the Museum of Modern Art. I walked into the Fauve Room and, suddenly, it came together. I felt a sense of warmth and tenderness in seeing the pink in relation to the green and all those pinks and purples. Although these were still lifes and landscapes, they were touching. The particular combinations of color made you feel the sun in a way that made you warm. I came back from the museum, got Woolard to look at the paintings, and after seeing them, he said, 'Yes, we need this warmth. We need to get the whole show brightened up a little bit.' So we did."

The give-and-take of designers includes, of course, the lighting designer as well. Along with creating the ambient and mood lighting for each scene and the pinball lighting effects—strobes, neon tubes and flashes—Chris Parry designed scroller lights to give the stage floor its color in keeping with the costume designer's color swatches. He, too, participated in increasing the saturation of color that underscores Tommy's traumatic state and the sense of his isolation from society. "I wanted to try and create a unique look for Tommy that would work especially well because he's dressed in white," Parry says. "So I established lighting angles with follow spots behind and on top of Tommy to create the kind of backlighting that created a sharp, bright outline around him." This outline motif interacts with and echoes Harrington's slide projections, and often throughout the production, Tommy is delineated in visual high relief against many backgrounds and situations.

Once the sets, costumes and lighting plots are designed or are in the process of design, there are myriad people who have to figure out how to achieve what the designers have envisioned. At this point the technicians take over.

The Dodgers' Sherman Warner and the technical supervisor, Gene O'Donovan, sat down early on with a budget and a wish list. They knew whom they wanted to hire to build the various components of the Broadway set, but they also knew they had to bring it in on budget and on time. "It was a horse race from start to finish," O'Donovan says. "We had only six weeks. But by keeping our eyes out for price and quality, we brought the set in for under a million dollars, which is pretty extraordinary for a show this complex."

"Complex" is an understatement considering the numbers of things that have to get done to make this show work. In addition to what is needed on ordinary large musical productions, this one needed multiple slide and video components—there are thirty-four video monitors and 2000 lines of computer programming for the video sequences alone, 2230 slides, eighteen slide screens

and fifty-four slide projectors for the back projections. This show was destined for endless technical rehearsals in order to get the elements to synchronize the way they must.

And after everything has been technically set in place, stage manager Frank Hartenstein becomes the master synchronizer. He has to move the show along at a seemingly, and sometimes actually, reckless pace. It's his job to make sure that the director's grand scheme is physically possible and probable, night after night.

Computers help, of course. But even computer cues have to be called, and there are usually not as many as there are in *Tommy*. Hartenstein calls a cue on the average of every six seconds, and, as he says, "Unlike most shows, in *Tommy* there's no margin for error. If you get behind on a cue, you'll never get caught up. It could be a train wreck." To avoid this, he spent six weeks in the rehearsal studio and six weeks in the theater working with the cast, carpenters, stagehands, electricians and the three other stage managers, Karen Armstrong, Jill Larmett and Kelly Martindale, to mark blocking directions and plot the show.

"I had to figure out all the fly cues indicating what piece moved when and do the same thing with winch cues," Hartenstein says. "We ended up generating reams of cue sheets that I could give to the flymen that showed

In order to guarantee that the choreography created before and during rehearsal will be transferred to the stage, every move is carefully blocked and marked on the floor of the rehearsal studio. Those marks are then recreated on the deck of the theater's stage for the final month of rehearsal. Before the first preview, all the marks are removed.

what each cue means, and we plotted out the entire show on the deck (stage floor) as well, and even did a timeline. Now on stage left they know that eight minutes into the show the bed's going to move off in track five, and they've got a minute and thirty seconds to take the bed out and put the exam chair on, or whatever the swap may be."

There is so much equipment and so little room backstage that only one act at a time can be on the deck, which means that while Act I is going on, Act II is suspended in the air in a cattle car. During intermission, Act I gets packed away and hoisted aloft while Act II is lowered into position. The pinball machines themselves are stacked up four deep and suspended on heavy chains above stage left and right.

The result of all of this hard work and meticulous planning is that *Tommy* moves with deceptive fluidity. But it takes sixty-seven people backstage (and banks of computers scattered about) to make that happen. There are 86 wigs—60 wig changes in Act I alone—225 costumes, 900 electric control channels and more than 700 lighting cues to be orchestrated for the show to run smoothly. Backstage traffic itself has to be choreographed so that dressers, wig changers and actors meet in the same place each night and stay out of the way of the prop people and stagehands. And they must all negotiate around those offstage voices connected to bodies that watch the conductor on the monitor backstage. (Space is even more limited because absolutely everyone, even the "star" has to stay off the bed which remains in the wings when it's not on stage; its white bedspread must appear pristine and unrumpled throughout each performance.) Although the wings can feel like an obstacle course, the actors and backstage professionals are adept at traversing it. They all know that being

"I'm constantly surprised by the fact that people love working on the show and they find that in their darkest hours, during the most exhausting rehearsals, the music actually is redeeming. And I think this is what makes music theatre so unique—good music won't redeem a bad story, or won't save a bad show, but if you've got a good show and a good story, it will lift it and make it fly."

—Pete Townshend

in the wrong place at the wrong time can create, if not havoc, an equally crucial second's lapse in timing.

Occasionally, of course, something can go wrong, but McAnuff and the two people who orchestrate the show each night from the overture to curtain down, Hartenstein and musical director Joe Church, have built in a safety net: "We were having some problems getting the pinball machine to come on stage at the right moment, so we built a vamp into the music," Hartenstein explains. "The same bars repeat over and over again until a specific cue happens, and then the musicians go into the next phrase of music. Joe watches, taking visual cues off the actors, and he knows that if he doesn't see the masking curtain go up to his left, it means the pinball machine is not moving. If he doesn't see it move at the end of the first vamp, he does another, and then continues to vamp until he knows the machine is moving. Once he knows the machine is moving, he can begin the top of "Sensation (Reprise)." One night the machine was really stuck, and it seemed like he vamped for three minutes. It was probably thirty seconds, but that's a long time to have nothing going on onstage. Paul Kandel as Uncle Ernie was standing there reading his newspaper, and at a certain point he just lifted it up to cover his face." But such glitches are rarities. For the most part the running time of *Tommy* rarely varies more than fifteen seconds.

If anything should go amiss, there is always another built-in safety and that's the camaraderie of the cast and crew. Having worked together for so long to bring *Tommy* to Broadway (many of the Broadway cast members were members of the original La Jolla Playhouse cast), they'll help each other out instinctively. The twenty-six actors-singers-dancers and five swings (those cast members who arrive at the theater every night in case one has to go on as an understudy) have gone through auditions, rehearsals, previews and opening night together. Maybe it's true of every cast, or maybe it's true because of the kind of show *Tommy* is, but they all agree that they are family—and they include in the kinship group every one of the people, onstage or off, who have made and continue to make *Tommy* an experience that brings cheering audiences to their feet night after night.

Rita D. Jacobs is a freelance journalist whose work includes A Day in the Life of America *and* From Alice to Ocean. *She writes for* The New York Times, *and* GRAPHIS *as well as many other magazines.*

STAFF

Book Directed and Produced by
Thomas K. Walker, *GRAF/x* and John N. Hart, Jr., *Kardana Productions*

Art Director
Thomas K. Walker, *GRAF/x*

Photography by
Peter Cunningham

Editorial Director
Rita D. Jacobs

Financial Director
Andrew Krivine, *Kardana Productions*

Editorial Manager
Victoria Hansen, *Kardana Productions*

Design Assistant
Sherri Whitmarsh, *GRAF/x*

Administrative Assistant
Peter Gardner, *Kardana Productions*

Research Assistant
Michael Wilson

Photography Consultant
Joe Standart

Project Advisors
Bill Curbishley
Nicola Joss

Agent
Jeff Stone, *A Stone Works*

Legal Advisor
Nan Bases, Esq.

Tommy Logo Design
Doug Johnson

Photographic Technical Consultant
CANON USA
Aaron Schindler, *Photo Perspectives*

The images in this book were photographed using the Canon EOS
Camera System supplied courtesy of CANON USA.

CONSULTANTS AND CONTRIBUTORS

This book would not have been possible without the generous
help of many people, especially the producers, cast and
crew of *Tommy*. Although it is not possible to name everyone
individually, we would like to thank the following:

Susan Allen
David Alpern
Jean Armstrong
Karen Armstrong
Richard Barnes
Helen Barr
Chester Biscardi
David Black
BMG Classics
Boneau/Bryan Brown
Early Boyd
Claire Bradley
Marvin Bromberg
Adrian Bryan-Brown
Sandy Carlson
Tom Carouso
Sage Carter
Chris Charlesworth
Anthony Chirico
Ed Cohen
Stella Connell
Lisa Cunningham
John Curley
Michael David
Sue Delaney
Tim Delaney
Barbara Dixon
Mike Drazen
Jim Dunnigan
Bo Eriksson
Bill Foley
Jane Friedman
John Frost
Fuji Securities Inc.
Kathy Gallagher
Doug Garland
Chris Gibbon
Nick Goderson
Janice Goldklang
Gary Gunas
Suk Han
Wendall Harrington
Jo-Anne Harrison
Benson H. Hart
Frank Hartenstein
Suzanne Herz
Ruedi Hofmann
Andy Hughes
Charlotte and Morris Jacobs
Jim Jerome
Doug Johnson
Altie Karper
Larry Kessel
Chip Kidd

Susan Kilpatrick
Emily King
Jill Larmett
Karen Lerner
Jacqueline Levin
Virginia Lohle
Nancy Lucas
Joan Marcus
Kelly Martindale
Maria Massie
Sarah McCraw
Sonny Mehta
Ina Meibach
Anne Messitte
Lisa Mordente
Ken Norwick
Gene O'Donovan
Robert Osborne
Jane Owen
Tom Pederson
Gabe Perle
Liz Perle
Abby Pollak
Lisa Portes
Denny Reigle
Dr. Clive Robbins
Bill Rosenfield
Joe Rosenthal
Neil Rosini
Pauline Rowlands
Nick Salisbury
Luisa Santillo
Ernestine Schlant
Wendy Schmalz
Ellen Schonfeld
Mike Schrom
Hellyn Sher
Beth Smith
Leslie Smolan
Anne-Lise Spitzer
Gary Stern
Ann Stratton
Ed Strong
Chad Sylvain
Susanne Tighe
Fran Trachter
Trinifold
Tim Trompeter
Shelley Wanger
Sherman Warner
Frederick Whittemore
Winterland Productions
Scott Zeiger

ORIGINAL BROADWAY CAST

Produced by
PACE Theatrical Group
Scott Zeiger, Gary Gunas
Dodger Productions
Michael David, Edward Strong, Sherman Warner, Doug Johnson
Kardana Productions, Inc.
John N. Hart, Jr., Mort Swinsky, Hugh Hubbard

Music & Lyrics by **Pete Townshend**
Book by **Pete Townshend and Des McAnuff**
Additional Music and Lyrics by
John Entwistle and Keith Moon
Choreographed by **Wayne Cilento**
Directed by **Des McAnuff**

CAST

Michael Arnold	*Local Lad/Ensemble*
Anthony Barrile	*Cousin Kevin*
Bill Buell	*Minister/Mr. Simpson/Ensemble*
Maria Calabrese	*Kevin's Mother/Ensemble*
Michael Cerveris	*Tommy*
Tracy Nicole Chapman	*Ensemble*
Paul Dobie	*Local Lad/Ensemble*
Jonathan Dokuchitz	*Captain Walker*
Tom Flynn	*Judge/Kevin'sFather/News Vendor/D.J./Ensemble*
Cheryl Freeman	*The Gypsy*
Jody Gelb	*Minister's Wife/Ensemble*
Christian Hoff	*2ndPinball Lad/Local Lad/Ensemble/Fight Captain*
Paul Kandel	*Uncle Ernie*
Donnie Kehr	*1st Pinball Lad/Allied Soldier/Local Lad/Ensemble*
Pam Klinger	*Mrs. Simpson/Ensemble*
Lisa Leguillou	*Nurse/Ensemble*
Norm Lewis	*Specialist/Ensemble*
Crysta Macalush	*Tommy, Age 4 Alternate*
Michael McElroy	*Officer #1/Hawker/Local Lad/Ensemble*
Marcia Mitzman	*Mrs. Walker*
Lee Morgan	*Lover/Harmonica Player/Ensemble*
Alice Ripley	*Specialist's Assistant/Ensemble*
Sherie Scott	*Sally Simpson/Ensemble*
Buddy Smith	*Tommy, Age 10*
Carly Jane Steinborn	*Tommy, Age 4 Alternate*
Timothy Warmen	*Officer #2/Local Lad/Ensemble*
Victoria Lecta Cave	*Swing*
Romain Frugé	*Swing*
Todd Hunter	*Swing*
Tracey Langran	*Swing*
Ari Vernon	*Tommy, Age 10 Understudy*
John Arnone	*Scenery*
David C. Woolard	*Costumes*
Chris Parry	*Lighting*
Wendall K. Harrington	*Projections*
Steve Canyon Kennedy	*Sound*
Batwin + Robin Productions	*Video*
David H. Lawrence	*Hair*
Steve Margoshes	*Orchestrations*
Joseph Church	*Musical Supervision and Direction*
John Miller	*Musical Coordinator*
Gregory Meeh	*Special Effects*
Foy	*Flying*
Steve Rankin	*Fight direction*
Frank Hartenstein	*Production Stage Manager*
Gene O'Donovan	*Technical Supervision*
Boneau/Bryan-Brown	*Press Representative*
David Strong Warner Inc. and Scott Zeiger/Gary Gunas	*Executive Producers*
The John F. Kennedy Center for the Performing Arts	*Associate Producer*
Mary Margiotta & Brian Chavanne (L.A.) Hughes Moss Casting (N.Y.)	*Casting*